Discourse on the Natural Theology of the Chinese

son antiquité establie en ... depuis
mille ans ou environ, ... longtemps ...
... temps avant la philosophie des Grecs ...
... Saincte Escriture ...
... ce seroit une grande imprudence et présomption
à nous autres, nouveaux venus ... sortis à peine
de la barbarie ... de vouloir ... une telle doctrine si approuvée
par ce qu'elle ne ... ne paroist point s'accorder
d'abord avec ... notions scholastiques ordinaires.
Je souhaitterois que nous en eussions les Memoires
plus amples et quantité d'extraits des Livres
classiques des Chinois, où ils parlent des principes
des choses. Mais cela n'estant point ... ne peut juger
... que par provision. Et comme le Père Nicolas
Longobardi second ... dire Longobardi, successeur Jesuite
... Vice-provincial ou directeur des Missions de la Chine, après le P. Ricci, qui estoit le premier
... du Père Matthieu ... et profonde ...
Mission, a esté un grand nombre d'années dans la Chine jusqu'à sa mort, estant presque à l'âge de 90 ans
et a rapporté ... de passages des auteurs classiques
Chinois, mais dans le dessein de les ... ce qui
... d'autant moins suspect ... de les avoir favorisés, j'ay cru que ce que
j'en tirerois pour donner un sens raisonnable
aux dogmes autorisés de la Chine ... qu'on ne
remarquera point ... sans une révolution, ... il n'y a point
d'apparence ... seroit servir plus seur, et ... joindray ... ce que le Père Antoine
... sujet ... une de la ... qu'il n'a adjouté
... Le premier principe des Chinois s'appelle Li (Longobardi §. 2. p. 13)
... c'est à dire raison ou fondement de toute la
nature (§ed. 9. p. 32) raison et substance universelle
(§ech. 11. p. 50) il n'y a rien de plus grand ... en ciel ...
... que le Li (§ed. 11. ... p. 53) ... Père
... de S. Marie Franciscain, ... a aussi ...
long temps dans la Chine, et a aussi ... escrit contre
leur dogmes des Chinois, dit ... que le Li est
la loy qui dirige les choses, et une intelligence qui
les conduit (p. 62) la loy et la regle universelle
selon la quelle le Ciel et la terre ont esté formés (p. 65)
Originel source et principe de tout ce qui a esté produit (p. 72)
il remarque que les Japonois disoient aux Missionnaires
que de la puissance et de la vertu du Li toutes les choses
... procedent comme de tous principe ... selon les Chinois
sans que le monde ait besoin d'aucune autre ...
le Li ... la seule cause qui fait mouvoir le Ciel depuis tant
de siecles d'un mouvement toujours egal il donne la
stabilité à la terre, il communique aux spheres la vertu
... leur semblables ... cette vertu n'est ...
dans la disposition des choses et ne depend point d'elles
mais qu'elle consiste et réside dans le Li, qu'elle predomine
... qu'elle ... dans tout ... gouverne et produit tout
d'un maistre absolu du Ciel et de la terre (p. 73) le Père de Sainte
... voilà le Texte Chinois dans leur philosophie ... livre 26 p 8

la quelle est pourtant
la première dont le reste de
... la terre ait des
ouvrages

il y a point d'apparence qu'on
... détruire cette doctrine ... une grande ...
... il est raisonnable de ... on ne pourra ...
également traduit

il seroit mesme à souhaiter qu'on
les fit traduire tous ensemble
y entrer

dans un petit ouvrage
imprimé (mais non
entier)

de les avoir favorisés, j'ay cru que ce que

cela ... grande et universelle
cause pure, qu'elle, subtile, sans ... et
sans figure, qu'il n'est connaissable
que par l'entendement (§ed. 5 p. 32) ... le Li
entant que Li
l'enten... en cinq
dans son traité sur
quelques points importans
de la mission
vertu, le ...
pieté, la justice, la
religion, la prudence et
la foy (§ed. 11 p. 49)

Pierre qu'il feroit un Jesuite.

le père de Sainte Marie ...
... liure 26 p 8

DISCOURSE ON THE NATURAL THEOLOGY OF THE CHINESE

Gottfried Wilhelm Leibniz

Translated, with an Introduction, Notes and Commentary

by

Henry Rosemont, Jr.

and

Daniel J. Cook

MONOGRAPH NO. 4 OF THE

SOCIETY FOR ASIAN AND COMPARATIVE PHILOSOPHY

1977

Library of Congress Cataloging in Publication Data

Leibniz, Gottfried Wilhelm, Freiherr von, 1646-1716.

Discourse on the natural theology of the Chinese.

(Monograph of the Society for Asian and Comparative Philosophy ; 4)

Translation of Lettre sur la philosophie chinoise à Nicolas de Remond.

Bibliography: p.

Includes index.

1. Philosophy, Chinese. I. Rosemont, Henry, 1934- II. Cook, Daniel J. III. Title. IV. Series: Society for Asian and comparative Philosophy.   Monograph of the Society for Asian and Comparative Philosophy ; 4.

B2591. L47E5 1977   181'.11   77-2411

ISBN 0-8248-0542-9

CONTENTS

ACKNOWLEDGEMENTS

These acknowledgements stand as testimony to the range, depth, and quality of Leibniz's mind: even with a division of the varied labors between us, much assistance was needed to complete and produce this work.

Our first debt is to Lynne van Voorhees of Lehman College, CUNY, whose detailed knowledge of 17th Century French syntax and idiom reduced markedly the number of errors from the first to later drafts of the translation; we are grateful for her close and careful reading of the text. John Tagliabue, of the Mittelateinisches Seminar, University of Bonn, assisted us in translating passages from Latin, and provided specific citations for several of the allusions Leibniz made to various aspects of Roman law and religion.

An early version of the manuscript was read by Eliot Deutsch of the University of Hawaii, Gerald Larson of the University of California - Santa Barbara, and David Mungello of Briarcliff College, all of whom made several helpful suggestions for improving it. The final version was given added clarity and detail thanks to a clear and detailed reading by Nathan Sivin of the Massachusetts Institute of Technology.

We are further grateful to David Mungello for making available to us the typed draft of his forthcoming Leibniz and Neo-Confucianism: The Search for Accord, to which we have referred frequently in the footnotes. Similarly, we

have frequently cited the German version of this work by
Renate Loosen and Franz Von Essen, <u>Zwei Briefe über das
Binäre Zahlensystem und die Chinesische Philosophie</u>; differences of translation and interpretation notwithstanding, we
have profited from the work of our predecessors. We have
also profited from the work of our contemporaries: Christopher
Benoit, Alan Berkowitz, and Thatcher Deane, of the Leibniz-
Bouvet Correspondence Project at the University of Vermont,
kindly made available to us drafts of their important work,
which we hope is soon published.

Because the monographs in this series are produced directly from a typescript, and because this particular manuscript
required several type faces, a planned layout, and materials
in several languages, it was essential that the final copy be
prepared with special care and skill. We are confident that
readers will agree that the work was done outstandingly well.
All of the credit goes to Anna Laura Rosow and Sally Warren of
the East Asian Research Center at Harvard University, who, in
addition to their typing, proofread the manuscript in an un-
commonly competent manner. Matching the typescript in its
aesthetic qualities is the Chinese calligraphy, for which we
are indebted to Diana Wang of the Korean Studies Department
at Harvard. Katherine Bruner, formerly with the Harvard University Press, kindly undertook the difficult task of pre-
paring the index.

Our final debt is to Albert Heinekamp and his associates at the G. W. Leibniz Gesellschaft in Hanover, West Germany, who supplied us, from the Niedersächsiche Landesbibliothek, with a photographic copy of Leibniz's autograph of the <u>Discourse on the Natural Theology of the Chinese</u>, and with other materials relevant to this translation.

To all of these people we are deeply grateful.

Lexington, Massachusetts   H. R.

September, 1976   D. J. C.

Discourse on the Natural Theology of the Chinese

INTRODUCTION

I. Background of the Discourse

If Erasmus of Rotterdam was the "Universal Man" of the late 15th and early 16th centuries, Gottfried Wilhelm Leibniz was a major candidate for the title two hundred years later. He not only studied, but wrote original works on subjects as distinct as geometry and biology, geology and theology, and metaphysics and statistics; his doctoral dissertation topic was jurisprudence; he was one of the foremost mathematicians of his time, and a famous philosopher whose fame has endured; and he was all of these while engaged in a long and active public career.

It is well known that China was among his many interests. He studied Chinese civilization throughout his adult life, and from the late 1680's until his death in 1716 his studies were fairly detailed, not merely exotic diversions. A significant amount of his correspondence was devoted to China, and several of his correspondents were among the most knowledgeable Europeans of his day on the subject of Chinese affairs. One of the relatively few of his writings on any subject published during his lifetime was his "Preface" to the Novissima Sinica (Recent News from China), issued in 1697 and again in 1699.[1]

A part of his interest was ecumenical; he wanted to bring together the several European countries into one Christian body, and he believed the goal would be realized sooner, and be more enduring, by including other major civilizations such as Russia and China in the expanded human community. But China was not only a means to an end for Leibniz, for he had a high regard for Chinese accomplishments in and of themselves, sufficient to think that China had much to teach Europe. In his "Preface" he wrote:[2]

> [I]f we are their equals in the industrial arts, and ahead of them in contemplative sciences, certainly they surpass us (though it is almost shameful to admit this) in practical philosophy, that is, in the precepts of ethics and politics adapted to the present life and use of mortals.

From the "Preface" alone, however, we will not learn about Leibniz's ideas on Chinese philosophy and religion in detail, because the bulk of the Novissima Sinica is more a catalog of current events dealing with China and the opening of trade routes than it is a serious sinological treatise. Further, although Leibniz regularly discussed Chinese thought in his correspondence, the discussions were usually only a few paragraphs in length. Not until the last year of his life did he set down his views on Chinese thought systematically, in a long letter written to one of his later correspondents, Nicholas de Remond, a French Platonist and the head of the Councils of the Duke of Orleans. In correspondence written the year before, Remond sent Leibniz two works on Chinese

religion written by Catholic missionaries, and asked the philosopher's opinion of them.[3] Leibniz's reply is the document
translated herein. It is usually referred to as the "Letter
on Chinese Philosophy"; Leibniz himself, however, referred to
the text as a "Discours sur la Theologie naturelle des
Chinois," which provided the title of this edition.[4]

Even by Leibnizian standards (and he was a prolific correspondent), the reply is a long one: over 14,000 words.
The main topics discussed are the Chinese conception of God,
universal principles, spiritual substance(s), souls, immortality, and the correlations between Leibniz's binary mathematical notation and the I Ching, China's oldest book of divination. In these contexts he also discusses his own famous
views of pre-established harmony, entelechies, primary and
secondary matter, and God. Further, he both states and shows
what he considers to be the proper method of philosophical
argumentation and demonstration in the Discourse, and, along
the way, makes repeated references to Greek philosophy, the
early Church fathers, and to history, both Western and Chinese.
The length and sophisticated content of the Discourse thus
make it a significant element of Leibniz's corpus, especially
when it is remembered that he wrote it in his 70th year; it
must be taken as a statement of the mature and considered re-
flections of the author.

It may therefore seem unusual that the text was not translated for two and a half centuries. A German edition did not

appear until 1966,[5] and the present work marks its first pre-
sentation in English. Part of the reason for this neglect
must lie in the fact that the <u>Discourse</u> was written in French,
which has remained a fairly common research language for scholars. Moreover, the text is by no means unique in being un-
translated; many of Leibniz's works remain available only in
the French, Latin or German in which they were originally
written.

But there are more substantive reasons for the neglect of
this document. First, while Leibniz had many insights into,
and understanding of, the history and nature of Chinese
thought, the <u>Discourse</u> should not be the only work read on the
subject. By the end of his life Leibniz was probably as well
versed on China as any of his contemporaries who had not actually been there; nevertheless, the <u>Discourse</u> contains mistakes, ranging from chronology, to authorship, to the meanings
of key Chinese philosophical and religious terms and ideas.
Most of these mistakes, of course, were not original with
Leibniz (he knew some characters, but could not read classical Chinese); rather did they come from the missionary writings
which formed the basis of much that he learned about China,
especially Chinese thought. These missionaries were the
ground-breakers of sinological studies in the West, guaranteeing that they would make mistakes even without the handi-
cap of bringing a strong Christian perspective to bear on the
non-Christian culture they were studying. If those mistakes

are now seen easily, the ease is due in no small measure to
the growth of scholarship that followed the early missionary
cultivation of the field.

Still another reason for neglecting the <u>Discourse</u> might
lie in the difficulties it presents to translators. In the
first place, Leibniz refers often and at length to the missionary writings, making it necessary to devote almost as much
time and energy to the latter as to the <u>Discourse</u> itself.
Cross-reading of this kind is particularly important for ascertaining the references to Chinese texts and authors, and
for determining responsibility for misspelled or mistrans-
lated Chinese terms, wrong dates, or clearly inadequate interpretations. Second, Leibniz wrote at times in non-standard
French, occasionally with archaisms and often with unusual
sentence constructions; while he wrote in a legible hand, he
made deletions and additions at the top of pages, at the bot-
tom, along the sides, and anywhere else he could squeeze in a
needed word or two.[6] Third, the transcription of Chinese terms
by Leibniz (and by the missionaries) is an orthographer's
nightmare. The original Chinese characters are not given in
the works consulted by Leibniz, and the missionaries were not
consistent in their systems of transliteration. Further, the
context of a passage usually does not make obvious which
Chinese terms are being transliterated, so that the various
Roman alphabetic spellings necessitate guesswork at times.
An illustration of these difficulties is seen in the <u>Discourse</u>

when Leibniz refers to a "Vuen-Wang" on one occasion, to a "Vuen Vuang" on another, and to a "Ven Vam" on still another.[7] In transliterating from Chinese into an alphabetic language consistency and precision in the use of letters and marks is essential, but all three quoted terms refer to the same person, King Wen, founder of the Chou Dynasty (1122-256 B.C.).

There is yet another reason, perhaps the most important, why the Discourse has not received more attention from scholars: the vision of Leibniz for a close understanding and communication between China and the West has not yet come to pass. The growth of knowledge of Chinese culture in Europe and the U.S. has not been matched by a similar growth in its dissemination, especially at the public level; and the respectability of narrow specialization in the academic disciplines provides a ready-made excuse for all but China scholars to professionally ignore the world's oldest continuous culture, inherited by one quarter of the human race. Nowhere else is this more true than in academic philosophy, where interest in the present document should be the greatest. If Leibniz's writings on logic, philosophy of science, and epistemology have been published in several editions, with many articles and commentaries on them, the attention reflects the concern of contemporary philosophers with logic, philosophy of science, and epistemology. If the philosophy and philosophical arguments of the Discourse are virtually unknown, with little written about them, then that, too, reflects something; and the reflection

is not flattering. In this light we would do well to heed
the prophetic remark made by Leibniz in a letter to Peter the
Great in 1716. If we do not actively promote understanding,
exchange and communication between the Chinese and ourselves,
he said,[8]

> It will follow that when the Chinese will
> have learnt from us what they wish to know
> they will then close their doors to us.

The Discourse on the Natural Theology of the Chinese should
thus be read by serious students of Leibniz, because of what
he said therein; and it deserves a wider audience as well,
because it represents the culmination of one gifted man's
efforts to keep a Western foot in the door, and to open it
wider so that we might all look in.

II. Sources of Leibniz's Knowledge of China

Almost totally ignorant of China for a thousand years,
Europe began to receive a trickle of information about the
"Middle Kingdom" again at the close of the 13th Century, beginning with the publication of the journals of Marco Polo and
his brothers. Nevertheless, knowledge of China was still minimal in Leibniz's Europe four centuries later; there were few
translations of Chinese texts, the language was considered
exotic, communications were poor and infrequent, and myths about
the country and its peoples abounded. For his information on
China Leibniz was thus obliged to rely heavily on Catholic

missionaries, who had been proselytizing in the country for
a little over a hundred years.

The five men most responsible for Leibniz's views on
China were Claudio Grimaldi (1638-1712), Matteo Ricci (1552-
1610), Nicholas Longobardi (1565-1655), Antoine de Sainte-
Marie (1602-1669), and Joachim Bouvet (1656-1730). Four were
Jesuits, the fifth (Ste. Marie) a Franciscan; all of them had
spent considerable time in China, knew the language(s) well,
and consequently were as well acquainted with almost all
facets of Chinese civilization as any other Europeans of their
time.

Although Leibniz had some familiarity with China early in
his life,[9] his mature study of the country and its culture can
be marked as beginning in 1689, when he met Claudio Grimaldi
in Rome. Grimaldi was born in Northern Italy, and took
priestly vows when he was nineteen. Entering China as a missionary in 1669, he soon found his way to the court at Peking,
and, with Ferdinand Verbiest S.J. ,(1623-1688), served as a
diplomatic aide to the Chinese emperor and became active in
the Jesuit mathematical and astronomical endeavors at court.
After seventeen years there, Grimaldi returned to Europe, and
met Leibniz at Rome in 1689.

Following their first meeting, Leibniz addressed thirty
questions about China to Grimaldi in a letter written in July
of the same year.[10] The questions ranged from the industrial
arts to botany, from chemistry to military weapons; they

reflect Leibniz's encyclopaedic mind, but also show that at
the time of writing he was not well versed in Chinese geography,
history or culture. Even at this early stage of his sinological development, however, Leibniz displayed the concerns that
motivated his later studies, concerns which he makes explicit
in the "Preface" to the Novissima Sinica and in the Discourse:
the importance of learning about China for Europe's benefit,
and the desire to increase Chinese receptivity to European
ideas and artifacts -- both concerns having as their goal a
closer cooperation, understanding and intercourse between the
two civilizations.

In answering Leibniz's questions   Grimaldi disparaged to
some extent -- not entirely accurately -- Chinese astronomical
abilities, which probably formed the basis of the philosopher's
fairly low opinion of the current state of natural science in
China.[11] Leibniz had a high regard for Grimaldi; partly because
of the latter's scientific skills, and partly because of Grimaldi's close association with Verbiest. The latter was also
a competent scientist, but more important for Leibniz's political concerns, was also influential at the court in Peking.
For these reasons, Leibniz and Grimaldi remained in correspondence for several years after Leibniz returned to Hanover,
and both Grimaldi and Verbiest contributed to the Novissima
Sinica. Grimaldi's influence on the philosopher was not,
however, confined to describing Chinese flora and fauna; the
missionary also held definite views about Chinese philosophy

and religion, views first put forth by the most famous missionary to China of the 16th and 17th centuries: Matteo Ricci.

The first Catholic mission in China was started by Ricci
shortly after he arrived in the country from Macao in 1583.
He remained in China until his death in 1610, and very few
missionaries before or since have learned as much about the
culture of the peoples whose conversion they sought.[12] Ricci's
command of spoken Chinese was excellent, matched only by his
skill in writing the difficult classical language. He wrote
literary essays which, from the standpoints of classical
learning, stylistic elegance and historical scholarship, were
virtually indistinguishable from the essays written by the
most prominent Chinese scholars and officials of his day.

Ricci's journals were published posthumously in 1620 under
the title On the Propagation of Christianity Among the Chinese,
with editions in Latin, Italian, German, French and Spanish.
The journals show Ricci's significant understanding (and appreciation) of Chinese customs, rituals and traditions, and argue
for the compatibility of these elements of Chinese civilization with the basic beliefs and practices of Christianity.
He excoriated popular Buddhism and Taoism, but cultivated the
literati (Confucians) that he met, whom he believed to be con-
vertible to the true faith because he also believed the classical texts which they revered could be shown to express ideas
consonant with Christian doctrine. More pointedly, Ricci
saw -- and the later history of missionary activity in China

showed the clarity of his vision -- that those classical texts
were a basic ingredient of a three millenia old cultural tradition, which was not about to be abandoned by intelligent
Chinese just because it was denounced by Christians, no matter
how scientifically knowledgeable, or courageous, or pious
those Christians might be. As a consequence, Ricci advocated
what came to be known as the "accommodationist" position with
respect to the conversion of the Chinese: tolerance for their
ancient writings, their ritual observances and practice of
ancestor worship, incorporating all of these into the Christian faith in China.

Although Ricci died before Leibniz was born, the latter's
admiration for the scholarly Jesuit is clear in the Discourse,
and it is Ricci's accommodationist position that Leibniz defends
and advances therein. Opposed to this position was Father
Nicholas Longobardi, who succeeded Ricci as the head of the
China Mission. Longobardi believed that the ancient Chinese
were materialists, and the moderns atheists; so that conversion
to Christianity required the renunciation of traditional
Chinese beliefs (largely Confucian). Unlike his predecessor,
Longobardi did not cultivate the Chinese literati to any great
extent. He believed that the basic tenets of Confucianism,
to which all educated Chinese paid at least minimal homage,
were flatly incompatible with Christian doctrine, and he set
down his views in De Confucio Ejusque Doctrina Tractatus (hereafter cited as the Religion Treatise).[13]   This work was

probably written about 1600, but not published until after the
death of Ricci, and it was not translated into French until
1701, well after Longobardi's death. The views expressed in it
were influential in undercutting Ricci's sympathetic approach to
Chinese conversion. The Religion Treatise is one of the two
works sent to Leibniz by Remond, and Leibniz's criticisms of
Longobardi's views are a major component of the Discourse.

Although Longobardi was one of the few Jesuits who disa-
greed with Ricci, most of the missionaries of other orders
attacked the accommodationist position, for political if not for
theological reasons. Prominent among them was the Spanish
Antonio Caballero, known also as Antonio Caballero a Santa
Maria, or, as Leibniz referred to him, Antoine de Sainte-
Marie.[14] This Franciscan, born in 1602, first went to China
from the Spanish mission in Manila in 1633, and left three
years later to take the anti-Ricci position to Rome. He returned in 1649, and remained in China until he died in Canton
in 1669. Shortly before his death Sainte-Marie wrote about
the Chinese Mission, but the Spanish manuscript now appears
to be lost. The French translation of the text was entitled
Traite sur quelques points importants de la Mission de la
Chine (hereafter the Mission Treatise). Published in 1701,
it was the other text apparently sent to Leibniz by Remond.

Like Longobardi, Sainte-Marie believed the ancient
Chinese to be materialistic (and superstitious), and their
successors devoid of spiritual views; therefore he, too,

advocated the need for total renunciation of China's tradition as a necessary condition for Christian conversion. Thus, Leibniz is no less critical of Sainte-Marie than Longobardi in the Discourse, and directs many of his arguments specifically to the Franciscan.

The position of Ricci with respect to converting the Chinese came to be the dominant one among the Jesuits, but it did not prevail in Rome. Opposition to this position was voiced by a few Jesuits, and by many Franciscans and Dominicans. The arguments lasted almost 150 years, and the "Rites Controversy," as it was called, was settled once and for all against the Jesuits by Benedict XIV's Ex quo singulari of 1742. The anti-Jesuit forces "won" the Rites Controversy, but "lost" the conversion of the Chinese; how much the loss was to be felt outside the Vatican will probably never be known. Had he lived that long, Leibniz would have been bitterly disappointed at the papal decision; in a letter written in 1710 he said: "In the Chinese controversy which is raging at Rome today, I favor the Jesuits and have for a long time. . . ."[15]

The last of the five missionaries who exerted a strong influence on Leibniz's views of China was Joachim Bouvet, one of the first French Jesuits to go there. Like Verbiest, Bouvet had access to the throne, and was a tutor of the K'ang-hsi Emperor's children. He entered China in 1688 and remained there for nine years, returning to Europe in 1697 to raise support (money and more missionaries) for the China Mission.

He had read the first edition of Novissima Sinica, and sent
Leibniz a copy of his recently published "Historical Portrait
of the Emperor of China." Leibniz published the "Portrait"
in the second edition of Novissima Sinica, and the correspondence between the two continued for awhile after Bouvet returned to China in 1698. The most significant exchanges of
letters took place from 1700 to 1703, after which Bouvet
stopped writing, probably due to the pressures of his work in
Peking. Leibniz's last six letters to Bouvet went unanswered,
which must have troubled the philosopher because of the intellectual excitement generated by their earlier correspondence.[16]

Bouvet thought on a grand scale, much more a philosopher
than philologist. He conveyed many original (and sometimes
far-fetched) ideas about Chinese history, language, and religion to Leibniz, three of which are reflected in the Discourse.[17]
First, Bouvet believed that the legendary early ruler Fu Hsi
("Fohi" in the text) had produced a notation for describing
all of science, a notation exemplified in the basic trigrams
of the I Ching[18] (see p. 20). These trigrams are made up of
combinations of solid and broken lines, but their scientific
and mathematical significance was, according to Bouvet, lost
on later Chinese, who simply saw the trigrams and their exten-
sions, hexagrams, as part of a system of divination. Second,
after learning of Leibniz's work in binary arithmetic, Bouvet
was able to translate the notation of Leibniz into the trigrams, as proof of his first claim. Leibniz's excitement at

Bouvet's letter describing the parallels can easily be ima-
gined, for the philosopher held firmly throughout his life the
belief that reason was all-persuasive, and if used by everyone, would eventually bring everyone to the true faith, i.e.,
Christianity. By thinking that the Chinese of 4500 years ago
possessed a mathematical notation similar to his own -- which
was useful for the exemplification of the principles of reason
-- Leibniz not only found support for his arguments that the
ancient Chinese had natural religion, but he was also able to
believe, thanks to his faith in reason, that the conversion of
the Chinese would proceed apace once it was demonstrated to
them that later generations had simply lost the true principles
set down by Fu Hsi.[19]

The last major idea of Bouvet's which is reflected in the
Discourse is more fanciful. Bouvet believed that Fu Hsi was
not Chinese, but a manifestation of the "Lawgiver," akin to
Hermes Trismegistus in the West; indeed, on the basis of some
questionable etymologies and arguments Bouvet even tries to
show that Fu Hsi and Hermes Trismegistus were one and the
same.[20] Further, according to the French Jesuit, the ancient
form of the Chinese language shows a relationship to ancient
Hebrew, and to the hieroglyphs of the Egyptians. Bouvet
promises to document these speculative claims in later letters,
but the documents are not forthcoming; the correspondence
from Bouvet's end stopped at this point. Yet despite what
must have been keen disappointment at having his later letters

go unanswered Leibniz gave credence not only to Bouvet's
views on the trigrams of the I Ching and binary arithmetic,
but to the Jesuit's views on the ethnicity of Fu Hsi as well;
although Bouvet's influence is seen most clearly in Part IV of
the Discourse, there are suggestions in the earlier sections
of the text that the founders of Western civilization (i.e.,
the "Patriarchs") passed on their traditions to the Chinese in
the dim past.[21]

    Leibniz's mature knowledge of China thus came primarily
from men who saw the country, its peoples and its culture
through the filter of their own culture, a situation that was
exacerbated by their avowed purpose in going to China: to
gain converts from the former to the latter. But their biases
notwithstanding, these men learned much of China, and the
three who advocated moderation and accommodation -- Ricci, Grimaldi and Bouvet -- came not only to have an appreciation of
the Chinese heritage that was uncommon among Europeans, but to
transmit that appreciation to Leibniz as well. As a consequence, Leibniz was opposed to the position of Longobardi and
Sainte-Marie, whose acquaintance with Chinese philosophy and
religion was not matched by any enthusiasm for it, and who
therefore argued that the Christian faith must supplant, and
not supplement, indigenous Chinese beliefs and practices.
Believing that this position was fundamentally mistaken, Leibniz wrote the Discourse as a rebuttal to the historical and
theological arguments put forth by the two missionaries in
their treatises.

The rebuttal rests largely on Leibniz's own philosophical ideas, and his own view of Chinese intellectual history, which caused him to distinguish sharply among and between the ideas of the ancient Chinese, and the Chinese encountered by the missionaries. In order to place the manifold temporal references in the Discourse in their proper context it is necessary to outline the order of development of Chinese thought, and Leibniz's views thereof.

III. The Chinese Intellectual Tradition

For purposes of understanding the arguments in the Discourse, the history -- real and legendary -- of Chinese thought must be divided into three discontinuous ages: 1) the era of the sage kings, from the 29th through the 12th centuries, B.C.; 2) the period of Confucius and his classical successors, from the 6th through the 3rd centuries B.C.; and 3) the "modern" period of Neo-Confucianism, with its criticisms of Buddhism, beginning in the 11th Century A.D. and continuing to Leibniz's own day.[22]

The Methuselah-like reigns attributed to them suggests that the earliest legendary rulers of China were just that: legendary. There is no evidence -- except for the legends, written millenia later -- that China was a major civilization circa 3000 B.C., the time period in which Leibniz (via Bouvet and others) places Fu Hsi and the oldest strata of the I Ching.

The earliest date in Chinese history confirmed by archae-
ological work is the 15th Century B.C., the period of the Shang
Dynasty, whose traditional dates are 1766-1122 B.C. The artifacts recovered from Shang sites reveal highly sophisticated
technological and artistic abilities in such areas as archi-
tecture, bronze-casting and writing, which show that Chinese
civilization, as a civilization, must go back to at least the
19th or 18th centuries B.C.; but this is still more than a
thousand years later than the dates accepted by Leibniz.[23]

Moreover, it bears emphasizing that there are no Chinese
texts which can be shown to be earlier than approximately the
11th Century B.C., and even these documents are fragmentary
and/or contain much material that was interpolated many centuries later. Thus, although the missionaries and Leibniz
refer to the sage kings as China's "most ancient philosophers,"
there are not even fragments of philosophical writings that
can be attributed to them.

In attempting to understand Leibniz's views of China,
however, the historicity of the legendary rulers is perhaps
less important than the qualities the legends attribute to
them. In addition to Fu Hsi, Leibniz mentions the emperors
Yao, Shun, and others, who share similar characteristics.
First, they were not supernaturally endowed; they lived to very
ripe old ages, but all eventually died, and during their life-
times performed no feats that contravened the laws of physics.
Second, the sage kings were highly intelligent, and they put

their intelligence to good use in the service of the Chinese
people by their inventions and discoveries (medicine, agriculture, writing, etc.). And third, the sage kings were moral
exemplars, endeavoring to rule by moral suasion rather than
force. From the Discourse it is apparent that Leibniz was
aware of these qualities, and he uses the morality and intelligence accorded them -- especially Fu Hsi -- in making his
case for the religiosity of the ancient Chinese. Indeed, his
highest praise for Chinese thinkers is given to these men.

After the period of the sage kings, the next significant
time period referred to by Leibniz (not always clearly) begins
many centuries later, with the birth of Confucius (551-479 B.C.).
No philosophical works prior to his time (if, indeed, any were
written) have survived, and there is little evidence that any
were extant during his lifetime. Works on other topics were
produced, however, and several of them have come down to the
present: books of poetry, governmental records, history,
rituals, divination, and so forth. Some of these works received special attention from Confucius and his followers, who
read philosophical and religious themes into them. These books
became classics (ching), and like the Iliad and Odyssey in
Greece, were not only a basic part of, but came to define the
later cultural tradition of the Chinese. Three of these
classics are cited specifically by Leibniz in the Discourse,
and thereby deserve specific mention.

(1) The <u>I Ching</u> (易 經), or <u>Book of Changes</u>.[24]
This book has several components, not all of which were written at the same time. The oldest strata are divinatory in
nature: symbolic descriptions of the 64 hexagrams which comprise the basic text. According to the <u>I Ching</u>, change takes
place in the universe because of the complementary interaction
of two fundamental principles, the <u>yin</u> and the <u>yang</u>. <u>Yin</u>
denotes passivity, receptivity, and descent, and represents
the female principle, the earth, darkness, valleys, moon, etc.
The <u>yang</u> principle is active and ascending, male, light, heaven, mountains and the sun. In the <u>I Ching</u> the female principle
is symbolized by a broken line (— —), and the male principle
by a solid one (——).

By means of a formulaic counting out of yarrow (milfoil)
stalks a person consults the oracle, obtaining at the end of
the count either a <u>yin</u> or a <u>yang</u> number, which is recorded as
a broken or unbroken line. The counting ritual is repeated
six times, until a hexagram (six lines) is obtained, and the
several female and/or male lines which make up the hexagram
represent, in symbolic form, the diviner's place in the universe at the time of consultation.

The hexagrams probably grew out of an earlier symbolic
tradition of trigrams (three lines), which represented familial,
social and natural phenomena. Thus, three consecutive <u>yang</u>
lines (☰) represented the sun, South, heaven, the head,
and the father, while three <u>yin</u> lines (☷) stood for the

moon, North, earth, the abdomen, mother, and so forth. One yang line followed by two yin (☳) stood for thunder, etc., and the oldest son; one yin line between two yang (☲) represented lightning, East. . . , and the middle daughter. Hence the hexagrams, read on the one hand as the sum of six lines, and on the other as being made up of two tri-grams, were replete with a metaphorical symbolism sufficiently rich that a good deal of concentration and meditation was necessary on the part of the diviner in order to determine the significance of the hexagram obtained.

As a consequence, the I Ching must not be seen only as a fortune-telling manual; no medium is needed to interpret the symbols, and the motive for consultation is not so much to pre-dict the future as it is to orient oneself properly in the natural and social scheme of things. Nor should the I be read as a proto-scientific work, in the sense that "science" is used today. It bears repeating that the yin and yang prin-ciples were seen by the Chinese as complementary rather than as antagonistic, and that these symbolized principles were not so much empirical explanations as they were metaphorical con-structs. As an illustration, a non-Chinese would probably symbolize peace, or stability -- using the I Ching paraphernalia -- as ☰☷ ; that is, heaven above and earth below. But remember that yang rises while yin descends, so that stability would be enhanced by having heaven below and earth above: ☷☰ -- the I Ching hexagram for peace.

The Chinese tradition -- passed on to Leibniz through Bouvet and others -- attributes the formation of the eight basic trigrams to Fu Hsi, circa 2800 B.C. More probably the oldest strata of the text date from about 1100-1000 B.C. at the earliest. In addition to the trigrams, hexagrams, and their descriptions, the Book of Changes also contains commentaries on them, and on the individual lines of some hexagrams. These commentaries were written much later, perhaps as late as the 3rd Century B.C., and are much more philosophical in nature than the earlier strata, without, however, altering the basically contemplative quality of the book as a whole.

In writing about the I Ching to Leibniz, Bouvet (and others) dismissed the symbolic and divinatory elements of the work, focusing instead on the sequence of broken and unbroken lines. For Bouvet,[25] these lines could be read in the first place as isomorphic with Leibniz's system of binary arithmetical notation, with 0 represented by — — , and 1 by ——— . Thus all of Leibniz's translations of numbers from base 10 to base 2 notation were similarly translatable into the I Ching notation of yin and yang lines. There is a way of ordering the hexagrams so that they can be read, using the Leibniz/Bouvet isomorphism, as an arithmetical progression from 0 to 63.

But Bouvet read even more into the trigrams: he saw them as the oldest form of Chinese writing, and, because he saw some similarities between the trigrams and ancient Hebrew (his correspondence does not say what those similarities are), he

assumed that in the very ancient past the Chinese had received
the culture of the West.[26]   Many of Bouvet's ideas would not
be given much credence today, but it might be noted that his
view of the trigrams as being the first Chinese writing does
have some traditional support.[27]   The tradition rests on the
fact that a few Chinese characters bear a resemblance to certain
trigrams (and hexagrams). The most striking example is the
character for water 水 , which was anciently written 〣
Turned horizontally with its lines straightened, this would
look like ☵ , which is the trigram symbolizing (running)
water in the I Ching.

(2) The Shu Ching 書經

Translated as the Book of History, or the Book of Documents,[28]
parts of the Shu Ching may be China's oldest written work,
dating from the 11th Century B.C. It is made up of a series
of small essays, memorials and documents which record parts
of the reigns of the sage-kings Yao, Shun, Yü, the reigns of
several Hsia Dynasty rulers, Shang rulers after them, and the
early years of the Chou Dynasty under Kings Wen, Wu, the Duke
of Chou, and their successors. It is by no means a complete
history of antiquity, and the oldest parts of it were written
down long after the events described therein were supposed to
have occurred. Further, several sections of the Shu Ching
were interpolated into the text at a later date, some of them
probably after the time of Confucius.

Although parts of the <u>Shu</u> are simply chronicles of events, other parts of it are the charges of rulers to their successors, or to their subordinate ministers, and the themes repeated in those exhortations had political and moral qualities that came to be definitive of the ideal Confucian state. Those in positions of authority were commanded to: (a) work for the welfare of the people; (b) maintain the rites and ritual observances of their ancestors; (c) be frugal; (d) view their position as a trust conferred by Heaven (<u>t'ien</u> 天), which was not so much a symbol of deity as it was a reflection of the natural order; (e) obtain and keep harmony within the social order, and between the social and the natural order. Many of the practices and ritual observances described in the <u>Shu Ching</u> were surely based on early beliefs in the supernatural, but these beliefs are not emphasized in the book, and were virtually ignored by Confucius and his followers during the classical period.

(3) The <u>Shih Ching</u> 詩經 , <u>Book of Poetry</u> or <u>Book of Odes</u>.[29] According to the disciples of Confucius, he regularly quoted lines from the <u>Shih Ching</u> to emphasize an ethical, aesthetic, social or political point he wanted to make. The original 314 poems which make up the book, however, are just that: poems; while some of them do indeed have morals that can easily be read out of them, the majority of them are celebrations of Chinese life. There are love poems, and poems lamenting a son or husband going off to war; poems dealing with

nature; with hunting and fishing; with friendship; with festi-
vals; and there are poems dealing with legends, and ancient
rituals. Together the poems of the Shih Ching paint what must
be the most accurate picture we have of the everyday life of
a Chinese living in approximately the 9th Century B.C.

Returning now to Confucius, he would probably have been
surprised to learn that the "Period of the philosophers" in
China begins with his birth. He said of himself that he was
a transmitter rather than an innovator;[30] a classicist rather
than a philosopher. This autobiographical statement is not
entirely accurate -- Confucius was an original thinker by any
standard -- but the statement does capture an essential ingredient of Confucianism: a deep respect and affection for the
rich cultural heritage of the past. He saw the ideal state as
having existed during the reigns of the ancient sage kings,
and advocated a return to their principles of government.
According to Confucius, (and the Shu, Shih and other early
works), the sage kings governed on the basis of ritual and
custom rather than law or force, were themselves reverent
toward the past, were more concerned to insure the material
and spiritual well-being of the people than in accumulating
personal wealth, and saw as their main task the maintenance of
harmony between the collective society and the natural order.

Like many other epochal thinkers of the ancient world,
Confucius never wrote anything that has survived. All that
we know of his views with assurance comes from the Lun Yü

(論語 often translated as the <u>Analects</u>;[31] Leibniz
refers to it as the "Lung Iu," "Lun Iu" and the "Su Lum Iu.").
The book is a collection of brief conversations between the
Master and his disciples, but other parts of the work may have
been written down a full century or so after Confucius died.
Many other writings have been attributed to him, and he is
supposed to have edited some of the classics; but it is now
widely held (as it was not during Leibniz's day) that the only
solid text for ascertaining the Master's views is the <u>Lun Yü.</u>

Most Western interpreters of Confucius, and not a few
modern Chinese themselves, portray China's First Teacher as a
thoroughgoing rationalist, agnostic in religious matters if
not downright atheistic. There is much textual evidence for
this view, some of which is not-too-enthusiastically cited by
Leibniz in the <u>Discourse</u>. Such a portrayal, however, can be
overdrawn; the "this-worldliness" of Confucius notwithstanding,
there are also significant passages in the <u>Lun Yü</u> which show
that he was at least occasionally concerned with less ration-
alistically-oriented issues. Thus, he is supposed to have
lamented that "Heaven had forsaken him" in one passage,
believed that Heaven had given him a special mission in another,
and in still others he was troubled by the fact that neither
in his dreams nor his observations of natural phenomena had he
been given a "sign" that he would be successful in his efforts.[32]

Such other-worldly concerns, however, are not the kind
Leibniz sought in seeking comparisons with Christian doctrine.

Interpreters of Confucius may never agree on the extent to
which he focused on the secular over the sacred, or the magi-
cal, but they all agree that he was neither a metaphysician
nor a theologian. The Lun Yü discusses ethics, rituals, customs, socio-political issues, and aesthetics in some detail,
but there are no discussions of first principles, God, primary
or secondary matter, Reason, and so forth; there are no dis-
cussions, in other words, of the major issues Leibniz discusses in the Discourse. It is for this reason that Leibniz
refers somewhat less to Confucius himself than to his legendary predecessors, or later followers, the descriptions of whom
can be more easily read as having Christian and/or cosmological implications, at least by stalwart readers.

The most famous successor to Confucius was Mencius, who
lived one hundred and fifty years later (ca. 372-289 B.C.).
In the book 孟子 that bears his name,[33] Mencius elaborated
the views of Confucius, and while he did discuss some of the
concepts taken up by Leibniz, for the most part the "Second
Sage" of Confucianism shared the non-metaphysical and non-
theological perspective of his predecessor.

Not until the Li Chi (禮記), or Records of Ritual,[34]
do we find a Confucian text that begins to link ethics and
socio-political thought with cosmological speculation (and
even in this book the speculations are not lengthy). The Li
Chi was probably made up in its present form during the 2nd
Century B.C., and the 49 heterogeneous chapters which comprise

it treat topics ranging from the details of social etiquette
to ontology. The book is fundamentally concerned with customs, rituals, morals and manners; one can find in it the proper
form of address to one's in-laws, sacrifices to be made by the
emperor, detailed instructions for bathing one's parents, and
so forth. Some of the chapters, however, attempt to link
these ceremonial duties with the place of human beings in the
universe, and two of these chapters were singled out centuries
later as worthy of especial study: the Ta Hsüeh (大學),
or Great Learning, and the Chung Yung (中庸), or Doctrine
of the Mean.[35]   The latter work is quoted several times by
Leibniz in the Discourse, as coming from Confucius; almost
surely it was written by some disciples(s) of his disciples,
but it is an authentic early Confucian work. In any event,
these two short works, together with the Mencius and Lun Yü,
are the "Four Books" to which Leibniz also makes reference in
his text. Taken together, these four works can be read a
variety of ways, but their basic thrust is clear, and can be
summarized succinctly by taking the lines from Pope: "Presume
then not God to scan // the proper study of mankind is man."

In summary, while classical Confucianism is correctly
characterized as religious and philosophical, the religion
is civil, and the philosophy ethical, aesthetic, and socio-
political. The very early ritual practices (of the Shang and
early Chou) inherited by Confucius and his followers were
originally derived from supernatural beliefs, but

those beliefs, while never repudiated, were nevertheless not
widely discussed by the educated during the period in which
he lived. No matter what his own personal views with respect to the supernatural may have been, Confucius saw that
those links with the rich cultural past were too important to
be lost in a secular age, and he therefore devoted his ener-
gies, as did those who followed him, to preserving those cultural links by placing them in a social and humanistic context.[36] With their steady focus on tradition, customs, rituals, rites and so on, the early Confucians laid claim to being
the guardians and transmitters of the Chinese heritage. It
is for this reason that ever since the classical period, referring to a person as a Confucian often meant little more
than that he was a typical member of the literati.

The third period of Chinese intellectual history significant for reading the Discourse begins over a thousand years
later. After many centuries of being eclipsed by the Buddhism imported from India, the Confucian classical texts under-
went thorough re-examination in the light of the changes in
Chinese thought brought about by Buddhist doctrines, and by
the changes in political and cultural patterns that accompanied
China's growth as an empire. This re-examination marked the
beginning of the period of Neo-Confucianism, and many of the
philosophers mentioned by Leibniz in the Discourse were forma-
tive of the renewal of the classical tradition: Chang Tsai,
the Ch'eng brothers, and especially the encyclopaedic

Chu Hsi (1130-1200).[37]   Taking some passages from the I Ching,
from the Mencius, Chung Yung, and from other classical texts,
the Neo-Confucians constructed a metaphysical system in which
to place the older Confucian concerns with moral, social and
political questions. Where the classical Confucians discussed
primary obligations, the Neo-Confucians discussed primary
principles; earlier critiques of benevolence and righteousness were followed by critiques of ether and matter; and
whereas the classical texts placed great emphasis on describing
the details of ritual sacrifices, the Neo-Confucians described
to whom and why the sacrifices were being made. This is not
to suggest that the Neo-Confucians distorted fundamentally the
views or writings of their forerunners. On the contrary,
they used their metaphysics to justify the earlier Confucian
way of life: spiritual self-cultivation could not proceed
without fulfilling one's many obligations to family and
society.

Neo-Confucianism came to dominate Chinese intellectual
life until the 20th Century. By the time of the Ming Dynasty
the history and philosophy of China as interpreted by Chu Hsi
became required reading for everyone, the Chinese examination
system being based on Chu's writings and commentaries on the
classics. In 1422 a major compendium of classical texts, with
the commentaries of Chu Hsi and many other Neo-Confucians,
was compiled. It was called the Hsing-li ta-ch'üan shu
(性理大全書   ; hereafter cited as the Compendium),[38]

and is the Chinese source most often quoted in the Discourse,
as it was by the missionaries Longobardi and Ste. Marie.
The form of the Compendium is partially responsible for the
fact that at times, Leibniz attributes views to philosophers
of the ancient period which were actually the views of the
Neo-Confucians. The anthology contains materials that span
twenty-three centuries, and neither Longobardi nor Ste. Marie,
who quote at length from the Compendium, always make clear
whether they are citing passages from a classical text or from
a commentary thereon. Indeed, parts of the Religion Treatise
and the Mission Treatise suggest that even the two missionaries are not always sure whom, or what, they are quoting;
this is especially true for Longobardi, who erroneously attributes much of the compilation of the Compendium to scholars
of the 10th Century B.C.[39]

The resurgence of Confucianism did not, of course, lead
to the demise of Buddhism, nor of Taoism, the second major
philosophical and religious tradition indigenous to China.
In Chinese religion, however, the several belief systems were
not as sharply demarcated, or as exclusive, as Western religious sects have tended to be. Depending on the locale, the
common people adopted different, but equally rich and complex
admixtures of beliefs, rituals, heroes and deities drawn from
Confucianism, Taoism, and Buddhism; sufficiently rich and
complex that sorting out the distinguishing features of each
school of thought was (and continues to be) a difficult task.

Moreover, by the time Father Ricci arrived in China to found
the first mission, there was a strong syncretic movement among
the intelligentsia as well, with many efforts being made
philosophically to merge the "Three Schools into One."[40]
This syncretism would leave Confucianism intact as a political,
social and moral code, adding to it substantive elements of
Buddhist and Taoist metaphysics, theology and liturgy.

But at the same time (early 17th Century), there were
many Chinese literati who were not religiously oriented at
all. They kept the official state and familial observances
prescribed by the Confucian classics, but were otherwise entirely secular, having little use even for the metaphysical
pronouncements of the earlier Neo-Confucians. It is partly
because of the views of such men that Longbardi, Ste. Marie
and other missionaries concluded that the Chinese had to
abandon completely their own ways of thinking if they were to
become true Christians. Leibniz did not hold these latter-
day secular Confucians in very high regard, made clear by the
epithets -- "Modern Atheists," "Sceptics," and "Hypocrites"
-- by which he referred to them in the Discourse.

In summary, it is essential to appreciate the peculiar
role played by Confucianism in shaping Chinese thought, culture,
and daily life as well. As a philosophy, with religious over-
tones, Confucianism was the dominant belief system among the
literate for most of the last two millenia. And because
governmental officials were drawn from the ranks of

the literate, Confucianism came to be the offical state ideo-
logy as well as the major intellectual force in China. Moreover, because Confucianism celebrated tradition, with all
its rituals, familial obligations, ancestor worship, etc., it
was exemplified in the lives of most traditional Chinese
commoners, who were thereby Confucians by practice even though
they had no first-hand acquaintance with the philosophical or
the traditional texts. Confucius, then, was not simply one
philosopher among many; his defense and enhancement of the
early Chinese heritage caused him to be seen as the symbol
of Chinese civilization, and he was consequently revered even
by those whose views were different (Taoists and Buddhists),
and by those who could not read the writings which contained
those views (the common people). Thus, the spirit of Confucianism was reflected strongly in the writings and actions of
Confucian philosophers, and in addition, it thoroughly per-
meated the entire fabric of Chinese culture.

Although Leibniz occasionally attributes a correct Confucian view to the wrong Confucian, and at other times attributes views to them which no Confucian held, he did appreciate the significance of the Confucian tradition in China.
Like Father Ricci before him, Leibniz also appreciated that
no other belief system would have an impact in that country
unless it came to terms with the country's intellectual heritage. He therefore wrote the _Discourse_, attempting to pour
some Christian wine in Confucian and pre-Confucian bottles.[41]

IV. Outline and Structure of the Discourse

For the most part, Leibniz describes his position and advances his arguments in the Discourse clearly enough to be
followed without undue difficulty. Nevertheless, a brief over-
view of the work may be useful, because the several historical,
philosophical and political issues at stake were not as
clearly delimited by Leibniz as a modern reader might desire,
owing in large measure to the fact that he was not only outlining his own views, but responding to the views of others.

The Mission Treatise and the Religion Treatise both make
the same arguments with respect to Chinese thought. According to Fathers Longobardi and Ste. Marie, resemblances between
Chinese and Christian concepts were only superficial, especially on issues basic to Christian theology: 1) the nature of
God, and spiritual substance(s); 2) the existence and qualities of spirits, and matter; and 3) the immortality of the
human soul. In the opinion of the missionaries the ancient
Chinese thinkers were, at best, materialists; and even this
much could not be said for their modern counterparts, who
were simply atheists. To support their position Longobardi
and Ste. Marie cited passages from classical texts, passages
from commentaries thereon, and they also quoted at length
contemporary Chinese intellectuals (some of them Christian
converts) with whom they had spoken. This evidence was
placed (according to Leibniz)[42] in a Scholastic philosophical

framework, from which their negative theological conclusions
are generated. And these conclusions in turn generate a more
political one equally negative: because Christian doctrine
is incompatible with Chinese thought, the conversion of the
Chinese can only proceed by having them abandon altogether
their intellectual and cultural heritage in favor of Revealed
Christian truth.

The Discourse on the Natural Theology of the Chinese is
an attempt to counter this position philosophically, and at
the most general structural level should be read as an argument modus tollens. The conclusion -- that conversion of the
Chinese requires abandonment of a 3000 year-old intellectual
tradition -- must be false; therefore the premise(s) from
which the conclusion follows must also be false.

There are four sections[43] in the Discourse, the first
three of which contain Leibniz's detailed replies to the missionaries' claims that Chinese thought is fundamentally incompatible with basic Christian doctrines. He first argues
(Part I) that the Chinese do indeed have a close conceptual
analogue to the Christian concept of God, and spiritual substance. In Part II, which is almost half of the manuscript,
Leibniz maintains that spirits and matter in China are considered and treated in very nearly the same way angels and
matter are considered and treated in Christian Europe.
Throughout Parts I and II, Leibniz's arguments regularly take
the form that first, Chinese thought is compatible with his

own philosophy; second, his own philosophy is compatible with
Christianity; therefore Chinese thought is compatible with
Christianity. Part III is devoted to making a similar case
for the compatibility of the Chinese and Christian concepts
of the human soul and its immortality.[44]

Together the first three parts comprise over nine-tenths
of the Discourse. Part IV appears to be more or less an
appendix to it, the subject under discussion being an exposi-
tion of Leibniz's binary arithmetic, and an analogue with it
claimed by Leibniz and Bouvet to be found in the trigrams of
the I Ching. Part IV is not, however, an appendix. On the
contrary, it is an essential ingredient of Leibniz's most
fundamental argument, and it must be seen as such in order to
appreciate Leibniz's overall view of the nature, history and
development of Chinese thought.

He accepts, for the most part, the claims of Longobardi
and Ste. Marie that many educated Chinese of his own time were
atheists. But, he insists, these moderns have "strayed. . .
from their own antiquity" (§1). If we focus instead on the
classical texts, he says, "I find [them] quite excellent,
and quite in accord with natural theology. . . . It is pure
Christianity, insofar as it renews the natural law inscribed
on our hearts" (§31).

To be sure, there are important theological issues on
which the classical texts are silent, and even the most famous
of Chinese philosophers, Confucius, is occasionally in

"error."[45] But this only shows, Leibniz believed, that we have not gone back far enough in the relevant cases. If we return to the era of the sage-kings, "we could uncover in the Chinese writings of the remotest antiquity many things unknown to modern Chinese and <u>even to those commentators thought to be classical</u> " (§68; emphasis added). The <u>I Ching</u> is one such book, according to him, and if we read it carefully, what we will uncover is the fact that "the ancient Chinese have surpassed the modern ones in the extreme, not only in piety. . . but in science as well " (§68a).

The crucial term in this quote is "science," which is why Part IV is crucial to the <u>Discourse</u>: "it concerns justification of the doctrines of the ancient Chinese and their superiority over the moderns" (§69). Remember that Leibniz acknowledged the theological weaknesses of modern Chinese thinkers, but maintained that the ancient texts -- some of them pre-Confucian -- strongly suggested a natural theology consonant with Christianity, and thereby worthy of European respect. What better way to establish that respect than to show that the most ancient authors of those texts not only had theological ideas similar to Christian theology, but also developed pure mathematics to a point which had only been reached in Europe during his own lifetime? Leibniz believed (as did Bouvet) that while binary arithmetic was not the "universal characteristic" he had long sought, it was nevertheless the basis of natural science.[46] If he could show, therefore -- to post-Galilean Europe -- that his mathematical notation had been prefigured 4500 years earlier in China, Leibniz would have a very strong case for denying the conclusion of Fathers Longobardi and Ste. Marie, and for advancing his own view of the proper method for engaging the Chinese in ecumenical dialogue: show them the truth, but not simply by quoting from the Bible and giving them telescopes; show them also how both theological and scientific truth could be read in their most ancient writings. (This argument also provided Leibniz with an explanation for the silence of Confucius on some important theological issues, and his "mistakes" on others; he, too, had occasionally lost the meaning(s) of the writings of his predecessors, and therefore could not be relied upon uniformly as the ultimate authority on, of or for Chinese thought.)[47]

Seen in this light, Part IV of the Discourse can be read as the coup de grace to the anti-accommodationist position with respect to China. The text breaks off abruptly, and although Leibniz continued to write for the remaining months of his life, he never returned to the Discourse to finish it. The evidence suggests, however, that philosophically, the manuscript may be substantively complete, and that Leibniz had accomplished what he had set out to do: provide a sophisticated philosophical and theological framework in which the ecumenical movement in China could go forward.

V. The Manuscript and Its Translation

During the later years of his life Leibniz maintained an intensive and extensive correspondence with Remond. The text now known as the Monadology was originally a letter written to the latter in 1714, and a little over a year later Leibniz began composing the Discourse, addressed to the same correspondent. In a letter dated 27 January 1716 Leibniz wrote that he had completed the work,[48] but two months later wrote to Remond again, saying, "I need more time to finish completely my discourse on the natural theology of the Chinese."[49] He never found the time, and the Discourse was never sent.

This translation is based on the original and only draft of Leibniz's autograph, to be found in the archives of the Niedersächsische Landesbibliothek in Hanover, West Germany, Ms. XXXVII, 1810, #1, entitled (by a later archivist) Lettre de Mr. Leibniz touchant les Chinois. No fair copy of the draft is extant, and several of the sixteen folio pages are frayed, making certain passages either illegible or incomplete. For this reason it has been necessary at times to rely on the earliest printed edition of the Discourse, which is found in C. Kortholt, ed., Leibnitii Epistolae ad diversos (Leipzig: B.C. Breitkopf, 1735), II, pp. 413-494. In the same volume Kortholt also includes the Religion Treatise of Longobardi (pp. 89-164) and the Mission Treatise of Ste. Marie (pp. 268-412) -- complete with Leibniz's footnotes on them -- which are the editions of the missionary texts that have been consulted and are cited herein.[50]   Having the

advantage of working from a fully preserved manuscript, the

Kortholt edition, despite many errors of transcription, is

the only source for some lacunae in Leibniz's manuscript.

The later edition by L. Dutens, G.G. Leibnitii: Opera Omnia

(Geneva: Fratres de Tournes, 1768), IV, 169-210, is not help-

ful in this regard because Dutens used the Kortholt edition

(and not the original manuscript) for his printing of the

text. Both Kortholt and Dutens entitled the work Lettre de

M. G.G. Leibniz sur la Philosophie Chinoise a M. de Remond.

Kortholt himself, like many early editors of Leibniz's un-

titled writings, is responsible not only for the title, and

the numbering of the paragraphs, but also for the division

of the manuscript into four parts, and their subtitles as well.

He also gave short descriptive titles (omitted from this

translation) to each numbered paragraph, inserting them col-

lectively at the beginning of each part.

Given the unsatisfactory and at times incomplete tran-

scriptions found in both of these editions, it is fortunate

that the recent German translation of the Discourse by

R. Loosen and F. Vonessen includes a new printing of the

French text as well. Their work is entitled Zwei Briefe

über das Binäre Zahlensystem und die Chinesische Philosophie,

which first appeared in Antaios, VIII (1966), 2, pp. 144-203.

The present translation differs significantly from Loosen-

Vonessen at times, both with respect to translations and to

transcriptions from the original manuscript. Nevertheless,
this German edition offers the best printing of the French
original at present, and the numbering of the paragraphs of
this English translation is taken from them; an appendix has
been added herein which gives all the variants where their
text differs from the original.

As a draft, hastily written and never completed, the Discourse suffers from many stylistic and orthographic inconsistencies. Except in passages deemed essential for understanding the text no effort has been made to be precise in the
transcription of Leibniz's manuscript in this regard. An exception is the transliteration of Chinese terms. While it
would have made for a smoother and clearer reading of the Discourse to have standardized, in English transliteration, all
of Leibniz's various spellings of the Chinese, it would have
attributed to him a familiarity with those terms which he may
well not have had. His Chinese transliterations, therefore,
have been transcribed precisely, so that readers of the text
may judge for themselves when, and where, Leibniz did or did
not know he was writing a variant spelling of the same term
he had used in another place. To compensate for this narrative difficulty each Chinese term (when known) has been
transliterated in the standard English form in the footnotes,[51]
and all variant spellings have been similarly noted and transliterated when they appear. In addition, the Chinese original
for each term mentioned by Leibniz is given on its first occur-
rence in the manuscript.

Leibniz's narrative inconsistencies and difficulties are
not confined to Chinese terms. It is clear that he did not
edit the text -- a simple arithmetical error of addition is
found in Part IV[52] -- and his French is often archaic and
opaque, abounding in many lengthy and convoluted sentences.
There being no point in translating vague French sentences
into confusing English ones, Leibniz's sentence structure has
often been modified in this translation, largely through the
use of colons and semi-colons, parentheses, and dashes. In
the few instances where there was an irreconcilable conflict
between his inadequate French and his obvious (from the context) intent, the latter has been determinate; what distinguishes Leibniz, and the Discourse, is his philosophical reasoning and not his literary abilities in a non-native language.
Whenever a linguistic liberty with the text has been taken,
it has been noted; for the rest, the careful Leibniz scholar
may consult the original manuscript, or the Loosen-Vonessen
transcription in conjunction with the appendix in this edition.

Many of Leibniz's citations to classical Chinese texts
are taken -- via Longobardi and Ste. Marie -- from the Compendium, none of which has been translated into a Western language. As a consequence, all references in the footnotes to
classical texts are to English translations (usually Legge,
who includes the original), so that non-sinologists may consult the sources as easily as Chinese specialists. On
several occasions a translation of a Chinese passage is

proffered in the footnotes which differs both from Leibniz's
text and from other English translations of the passage; all
such occasions are marked, followed by reference(s) to other
translations.

The translators' own general interpretations of Leibniz's
views, and of Chinese thought, are contained in this Introduction. More specific interpretations are also given in the
footnotes, but an effort has been made to keep the notes
basically factual when possible, because the Discourse has
been sufficiently neglected by scholars that it would be pre-
mature, and perhaps stultifying, to attempt to impose a be-all
and end-all reading of the text at the present time; the goal
of this first English edition has been merely to provide a
useful begin.[53]

FOOTNOTES TO THE INTRODUCTION

1.   Donald F. Lach, trans., <u>The Preface to Leibniz' NOVISSIMA SINICA</u>,
hereafter referred to as Lach (1). His edition is based on the 1699
printing.

2.   Lach (1), p. 69.

3.   The two texts discussed by Leibniz in the <u>Discourse</u> were written by
Fathers Longobardi and Ste. Marie, to be taken up in detail later in this
Introduction. In his letters to Leibniz of 1 April and 4 September 1715,
Remond mentions the Longobardi work, but not Ste. Marie's, mentioning
instead Nicholas Malebranche (1638-1715), who wrote <u>A Dialogue Between a
Christian Philosopher and a Chinese Philosopher: On the Existence and
Nature of God</u> (Paris, 1708). Receipt of this latter work is acknowledged
by Leibniz, even though it is never cited in the <u>Discourse</u>. Leibniz
must have received the Ste. Marie text from Remond as well however, because
he acknowledged it in a letter of 4 November 1715: "It would now remain
to speak to you sir, of the natural theology of the Chinese literati,
according to what the Jesuit Father Longobardi and Father Antoine de
Ste. Marie, of the Minorite order, report to us thereon in the treatises
which you have sent me, . . ."   Remond's letter of 1 April is in Gerhardt
III, p. 640; the letter of 4 September, <u>Ibid</u>., p. 651; Leibniz's letter
of 4 November, <u>Ibid</u>., p. 660. An English translation of Malebranche's
<u>Dialogue</u> has recently been completed by George Stengren of Central Michi-
gan University.

4.   In his letter to Remond of 27 March 1716. Gerhardt III, p. 675.
Similarly, in a letter of 13 January 1716 written to Bartholomew des Bosses
S.J., with whom Leibniz corresponded in Latin, he referred to his manuscript as a "dissertationem de Theologia Sinensium naturali." Gerhardt
II, p. 508. From his earlier correspondence with des Bosses it is clear
that Leibniz knew something of the works of Longobardi and Ste. Marie
before receiving them from Remond, because he mentions reading reviews of
them in 1709. See Gerhardt II, p. 380-81.

5.   See p. 40.

6. The Frontispiece in this edition is a copy of Leibniz's folio page 1 verso, reproduced from the copy of the entire manuscript provided through the courtesy of the G.W. Leibniz Gesellschaft in Hanover.

7. In §34, §58 and §68 respectively.

8. Translated in Wiener, p. 598.

9. Lach (2), p. 439.

10. A copy is in the Grimaldi-Leibniz file, Leibnizbriefe 330, #3-5, in the Niedersächische Landesbibliothek with the date of 19 July 1689. The correspondence between Grimaldi and Leibniz has not been published; for a fuller discussion of the contents of their letters, see Mungello, Chapter 4, and Lach (1), pp. 11-12 and passim.

11. Fn. 10. A fuller account of Western astronomy in China is in Sivin.

12. Joseph Needham, for example, calls Ricci "one of the most remarkable and brilliant men in history." Needham, vol. 1, p. 148.

13. Translated in French as Traite Sur Quelques Points de la Religion des Chinois; see p. 11 below. Referring to the works of Longobardi and Ste. Marie as the Religion Treatise and the Mission Treatise, respectively, was first done by Mungello, and the same abbreviations are retained here to facilitate cross-references with his work.

14. About Antoine de Sainte-Marie nothing is known. His name cannot be found in other materials pertaining to Leibniz (except as the author of the Mission Treatise), nor in French biographical dictionaries, nor in Catholic dictionaries and encyclopaedias. There are several references, however, in these works to a Spanish Franciscan named Antonio Caballero, who is also called therein Antonio Caballero a Santa Maria. The dates and activities given and described for Caballero correspond precisely with those that must be assumed for Ste. Marie on the basis of statements and dates found in the Mission Treatise. Moreover, the epitaph in Canton included in Caballero's most detailed biography reads (with thanks to our student Freddie Vasquez for assistance with Spanish passages):

A. R. P. F. ANTONIO A S. MARIA

ORDINIS MINORUM, MINISTRO ET PRAEFECTO VERE APOSTOLICO

AB EXILIO CANTONENSI AD COEL ESTEM PATRIAM EVOCATO

ANNO M. D. C. L. XIX.

-- which suggests strongly that Caballero and Ste. Marie were one and
the same. The biographies of Caballero do not, however, specifically mention his writing the Mission Treatise, so there remains some room for
doubt. See Sinica Franciscana, vol. II, p. 329, and the New Catholic Encyclopaedia under "Caballero."

15. Gerhardt III, p. 549; cited also in Lach (2), p. 447.

16. See H. Wilhelm (1). See also Mungello, who devotes the third chapter of his work to the Leibniz-Bouvet correspondence.

17. Several commentators have implied that the isomorphism of his binary
system and the trigrams of the I Ching was discovered by Leibniz and transmitted to Bouvet. Thus Lach (2), p. 446, says: "By his analysis of Fu
Hsi's trigrams, Leibniz hoped to strengthen Father Bouvet's theory that
the I Ching was a key to all the sciences." There is certainly some support for this view, for Leibniz himself said as much. In his letter to
Tsar Peter, for example, he said: "The new and marvelous discovery I have
made, namely, the secret of deciphering the old characters of the famous
Fohi. . . ." Wiener, p. 598. But Bouvet's letter to Leibniz of 4 November 1701 shows fairly clearly that Leibniz provided Bouvet with an outline of his binary system, and that the missionary provided the hypothesis
of the isomorphism of it with the I Ching trigrams. And at other times
Leibniz himself acknowledges Bouvet's work on this issue, as in a paper
he published in 1703 (see textual fn. 188). See also Needham, II, p. 341.

18. See also Waley (1).

19. See pp. 36-38.

20. Bouvet to Leibniz, 4 November 1701. See fn. 17 above, and textual
fn. 79.

21. I.e., in §24, §32, and §37. See also Merkel, pp. 83-84.

22. This temporal trichotomy is by no means the invention of Leibniz; most Chinese of the Confucian persuasion, from at least the 12th through the late 19th centuries, would have outlined the intellectual history of their civilization in roughly the same way.

23. The most recent study of the Shang Dynasty is Keightley. While the Shang had a sophisticated writing system, all extant materials are in the form of brief divinatory formulae, or memorials; no texts, if any were written, have been unearthed.

24. The best translation of which is R. Wilhelm. See also H. Wilhelm (2).

25. Bouvet to Leibniz, 4 November 1701. See also fn. 17, above, and textual fn. 79.

26. *Ibid*.

27. Although Fu Hsi is known as the inventor of the trigrams, the tradition usually accords the honor for the invention of writing per se to the Yellow Emperor's minister Ts'ang Chieh 倉頡 , ca. the 27th Century B.C.

28. Translated in Legge, vol. III, and Karlgren (2).

29. Legge, vol. IV. A more poetic translation is Waley (2), and the most literal translation is Karlgren (3).

30. *Lun Yü* 7:1. All references to the *Lun Yü* here and in the textual notes are by book and chapter number. For other translations see Legge, vol. I, and Waley (3), both of which use the same numbers employed herein.

31. See fn. 30.

32. *Lun Yü* 11:7, 7:22 and 9:5, 7:5, and 9:8 respectively.

33. Translated in Legge, vol. II.

34. Translated in Legge/Chai.

35. Chapters 39 and 28.

36. An original philosophical interpretation of Confucius in this context is found in Fingarette. See also the review article of Fingarette in Rosemont. Another interpretation is in Creel.

37. These Neo-Confucians are taken up in the textual notes. See also Bernard.

38. Mungello uses the Compendium to refer to the Hsing-li ta-ch'üan shu, and again, the term is kept herein to facilitate cross-references with his work. For the difficulties faced by the missionaries and Leibniz in citing this work accurately see Mungello, esp. Chapter 5.

39. Religion Treatise (1;9). In his marginal notes to Longobardi's text Leibniz makes reference to Ste. Marie's bibliographic discussion, who placed the compilation of the Compendium as occurring 300 rather than 2500 years earlier.

40. Efforts to combine the san chiao 三教 , "Three Teachings," can be traced to the 11th Century, and it became a significant movement by the 14th, in Ming times. Arthur Wright has argued that many Chinese emperors endorsed the syncretism as a means of increasing social control. Wright, pp. 100-101. This may help to explain why many Neo-Confucians of the late Ming and early Ch'ing struggled to keep their belief system free of the "impurities" of Taoism and Buddhism; see, for example, W.T. de Bary.

41. As mentioned earlier, the Neo-Confucians did not break with their classical predecessors. Rather did they add to the early works, especially in the areas of cosmology, ontology and epistemology. One of the major threads which ties both traditions together is the importance of self-cultivation, not only for moral strength, but for spiritual insight as well. The discipline involved in self-cultivation takes on a contemplative element in Neo-Confucianism which is not found in the classical tradition to any extent, but the emphasis on self-cultivation and personal discipline is constant. In the Discourse Leibniz does not show that he is aware of this central thread of all Confucianism. But neither do Longobardi and Ste. Marie, and Leibniz is not so much concerned in the Discourse to explicate Confucianism in full as he is to counter the attacks of the missionaries. See also Bodde, and Schwartz.

42. See esp. §39 and §39a.

43. The formal sectioning was done by Kortholt, but is not misleading;

Leibniz described the _Discourse_ in a way parallel to the sections in a
letter to Remond of 17 January 1716. Gerhardt III, p. 665.

44. Leibniz also employs regularly two other forms of argument in the
Discourse: 1) when confronted by a Chinese passage which appears to be
clearly in conflict with Christian theology, Leibniz attempts to show that
similar "errors" had been made by the Greeks, or early Church Fathers,
scholastics, etc., without destroying Christianity, or indeed, without
diminishing the respect with which such persons were treated in the
Western tradition; 2) when rebutting a specific charge of Longobardi and/
or Ste. Marie against the ancients, Leibniz will point out whenever possible that the ancient texts do not explicitly state the heresy charged by
the missionaries. Whatever the persuasiveness of these particular arguments from negative evidence may have been in his own day, they cannot be
given credence today, because most of the "heresies" deal with metaphysical and/or theological issues which were not discussed in the ancient
texts at all. There being no statements about prime matter in the classical texts, for example, it follows trivially, but worthlessly, that there
cannot be any statements in the classical texts which contradict Christian statements about prime matter.

45. As, e.g., in §49 and §50.

46. Bouvet's letter of 4 November 1701 suggests this view for Leibniz's
binary system, and in his letter of 8 November 1702 says that the same
system, as embodied in the trigrams of the _I Ching_, was the basis (now
lost) of music, physics, and so forth, as well as arithmetic for the
ancient Chinese. See also Mungello, Chapter 3.

47. In §49 Leibniz says that "Confucius himself could have been ignorant
about that which he did not want to investigate more deeply."

48. Gerhardt III, p. 667.

49. _Ibid._, p. 675.

50. Kortholt calls this section of the volume "Anciens Traitez de divers
auteurs sur les ceremonies de la Chine avec des notes de Monsieur de
Leibniz."

51. With reluctance, the Wade-Giles system of Romanization is used throughout, instead of the pin yin system now standard in the People's Republic of China. On the one hand, whenever the Chinese original is available Chinese specialists do not need any Romanization at all. On the other hand, non-sinologists who wish to consult English works on Chinese philosophy and religion will confront the Wade-Giles system, and to have added still one more kind of spelling to the many already present in this text would have made a difficult task virtually impossible.

52. See textual fn. 197.

53. Minor textual matters: 1) as noted above, parentheses have been employed on occasion to simplify Leibniz's own language, but all materials enclosed in square brackets have been interpolated by the translators; 2) Leibniz's textual references to Longobardi and Ste. Marie have been made uniform, with the former cited by both a section and a page number, separated by a full colon, and the latter cited by page number only; and 3) citations in the footnotes are by author, with a full citation for each consulted work appearing in the Bibliography.

DISCOURSE ON THE NATURAL THEOLOGY OF THE CHINESE

Monsieur [Remond]:

[I. Chinese Opinion Concerning God]

§1   I have taken the pleasure of looking through the books
you sent me on Chinese thought.   I am inclined to believe
that the [Chinese] writers, especially the ancient ones,
make much sense.   There should be no difficulty in granting
that to them despite the opinions of some of their own modern
writers.   It is comparable to the Christians, who are not
always obliged to follow the meaning which the Scholastics
and later commentators have given to Scripture, the Church
Fathers or the ancient laws.   A fortiori, concerning the
Chinese, where the Monarch, who is the leader of all sages
and the living embodiment of the law, appears to reveal
national expressions of ancient doctrines.[1]   Therefore the

---

1.   Leibniz's reference to the Chinese monarch here and two sentences
below is to the K'ang Hsi (康熙) Emperor, who reigned from 1662-1722.
During Longobardi's time, China was suffering from the internecine wars
that eventuated in the overthrow of the Ming Dynasty (1368-1644).   The
new Ch'ing, or Manchu Dynasty (1644-1911), brought a new stability to
China, reflected in the length of K'ang Hsi's reign: 61 years.

grounds upon which Father Nicholas Longobardi (successor to Father Ricci, founder of the mission to China) most often supports himself in order to combat the accommodationist explanations of his predecessor, namely, that the Mandarins did not take such ancient writings seriously (something which made for considerable difficulty in Ricci's time), are no longer valid today by authority of this prince and many knowledgeable members of his court. One should therefore profit from so great an authority. It is the proper way of correcting quite subtly, without appearing to do so, those who have strayed from the truth and even from their own antiquity. This shows that one should not be put off initially by such difficulties and that Father Martinius[2] and those who are of his opinion, have done wisely to follow the advice of Father Ricci and other great men, and to maintain these explanations in spite of the opposition of Father Emanuel Diaz, S.J.,[3] Father Nicholas Longobardi, S.J., and

---

Although the Emperor exercised firm control over the government, he was an excellent scholar and patron of the arts. Leibniz was very impressed with the K'ang Hsi Emperor, as his flattering remarks here and in the "Preface" to the Novissima Sinica make clear. See Lach (1), esp. pp. 71-74.

2. Martino Martini (1614-1661), a Jesuit missionary in China. His trip to Rome (c. 1650) was influential in obtaining official papal support for the Jesuit (Ricci's) position on the Rites Controversy.

3. Like Longobardi, Emanuel Diaz (1574-1659) was one of the few Jesuits who had little use for Chinese thought and ritual practices. He wrote on astronomy for the Chinese court.

of Father Antoine de Sainte-Marie Franciscan, and in spite of
the contempt of several Mandarins. It would be enough for
the explications of the ancients simply to be sustainable because the opinions of modern Chinese appear to be ambivalent.
But to examine these things more closely, these explications
can, in fact, be more than sustained by the texts.[4] I speak
here only of doctrine and will not examine ceremonies or worship, which require longer discussion.

§2   Initially, one may doubt if the Chinese do recognize,
or have recognized, spiritual substances. But upon reflection, I believe that they did, although perhaps they did not
recognize these substances as separated, and existing quite
apart from matter.[5]   There would be no harm in that with regard to created Spirits, because I myself am inclined to
believe that Angels have bodies; which has also been the
opinion of several ancient Church Fathers.[6] I am also of the

---

4.   I.e., passages from Chinese texts translated and quoted in the
treatises of Longobardi and Ste. Marie.
5.   A theme developed further in §40 and §41.
6.   The existence of the Devil and "fallen" angels is explained by several early Church Fathers as showing that certain orders of angels must
possess some sort of material body, and thus, not being "essentially
good," are capable both of good and evil. For example, Origen, De
Principiis, I, v, 1-3; St. Justin (Martyr), The Second Apology, 5. St.
Justin is quite explicit, calling the Biblical manna "angel's food" (Dialogue with Trypho, 57). St. Augustine speculated that God communicates

opinion that the rational soul is never entirely stripped of all matter.[7] However, with regard to God, it may be that the opinion of some Chinese has been to give Him a body, to consider God as the Soul of the World, and to join God to matter, as the ancient philosophers of Greece and Asia have done. But in showing that the most ancient authors of China attributed to the Li,[8] or first principle, the production

---

corporeal actions through the medium of angelic bodies (On the Trinity, III, x, 21) and that the bodies of evil angels never die (Enchiridion, XXV, XXVI). Lactantius also believed that angels and human souls are of a heavenly fire -- following Psalm 104.4. See §63.

7. In §47 below, Leibniz states that there are an infinity of animated or ensouled substances, below as well as above the soul of man. The superhuman souls or spirits are called "genii," or more traditionally, "angels." No soul, whether animal, human or superhuman is ever entirely separated from a body, even if it is a very subtle or ethereal one (§14, 20, 63), or, in a religious sense, made up of celestial fire or ether (§63, 64; see fn. 6). There are no "totally separate souls, nor genii without bodies. God alone is entirely bodiless." (Monadology, #72). Leibniz is always quick to note that this does not mean that a soul is nothing but an accidental collocation of material atoms (§21) or merely the epiphenomenon of some changing and perishable material substratum (§60; cf. Plato's doctrine in the Phaedo). For the reason why Leibniz held the view that "the rational soul is never entirely stripped of all matter," see fn. 135.

8. Li 理 , "Principle," "Reason." In §14 Leibniz discusses the etymology of this term. See fn. 44. For a history of the development of this concept in Neo-Confucianism, see Wing-tsit Chan.

itself of the Ki,[9] or matter, one need not reprimand them,
but simply explain them. It will be easier to persuade
their disciples that God is an Intelligentia supramundana,
and is superior to matter. Therefore, in order to determine whether the Chinese recognize spiritual substances,
one should above all consider their Li, or order, which is
the prime mover and ground of all other things, and which I
believe corresponds to our Divinity. Now it is impossible
to understand this [correspondence] with reference to a
thing purely passive, brutish and indifferent to all, and
consequently without order, like matter. For example, internal order comes not from wax itself, but from whoever
forms it. Also, their Spirits, which they [the Chinese]
attribute to the elements, to the rivers, and to the mountains, represent either the power of God who appears through
them, or perhaps (according to the opinion of some of them),
they represent particular spiritual substances which are
endowed with the force of action and with some knowledge,
although they attribute subtle and ethereal bodies to them
like the ancient philosophers and [Church] Fathers attributed to genii or Angels. That is why the Chinese are
like those Christians who believed that certain Angels

---

9. Ch'i 氣 , "Ether," "air," "breath," "force," "matter." Originally
used to denote the elan vital in human beings (as, e.g., in the Mencius),
ch'i was developed by the Neo-Confucians as the complement (matter/force)
of li (form/principle).

govern the elements [of earth] and the other large bodies;[10]
which would be an obvious error, but which would not overthrow Christianity. During the time of the Scholastics,
one did not condemn those who believed, with Aristotle, that
certain intelligences governed the celestial spheres. Those
among the Chinese who believe that their ancestors and great
heroes are among the Spirits, come rather close to the words
of our Lord [Matt. 22:30] which suggest that the Blessed
resemble the Angels of God. It is then important to consider that those who give bodies to the genii or Angels,
like the ancient philosophers or early Fathers, do not thereby deny the existence of created spiritual substances, for
they accord rational souls to these genii endowed with
bodies, as also men have them, but souls more perfect because their bodies are also more perfect. Therefore, Father
Longobardi -- and Father Sabbatini[11] who is cited by him --

---

10. For example, Origen, whom Leibniz mentions below in another context (§60) believed that God appointed certain angels to administer the
natural elements:

> For we say that the earth bears the things which are said
> to be under the control of nature because of the appoint-
> ment of invisible husbandmen, so to speak, and other gov-
> ernors who control not only the produce of the earth but
> also all flowing water and air. Contra Celsum, VIII, 31.

11. Sabatino De Ursis, S.J. (1575-1620), a colleague of Ricci and Longobardi in Peking. He wrote the first treatise on the Chinese calendar
in a Western language, which is translated in D'Elia.

should not conclude from the fact that the Chinese appear to
attribute bodies to their Spirits, that they do not at all
recognize the existence of spiritual substances.

§3   China is a great Empire, no less in area than cultivated Europe, and indeed surpasses it in population and
orderly government. Moreover, there is in China in certain
regards an admirable public morality conjoined to a philosophical doctrine, or rather doctrine of natural theology,
venerable by its antiquity, established and authorized for
about 3000 years,[12] long before the philosophy of the Greeks
whose works nevertheless are the earliest which the rest
of the world possess, except for our Sacred Writings. For
both of these reasons, it would be highly foolish and pre-
sumptuous on our part, having newly arrived compared with
them, and scarcely out of barbarism, to want to condemn
such an ancient doctrine because it does not appear to
agree at first glance with our ordinary scholastic notions.
Furthermore, it is highly unlikely that one could destroy
this doctrine without great upheaval. Thus it is reasonable to inquire whether we could give it a proper meaning.
I only wish that we had more complete accounts and greater

---

12. This reference to a 3000-year old doctrine of natural theology,
coupled with Leibniz's high admiration for the trigrams of the I Ching,
suggest that it is probably this classical text to which he is alluding.

quantity of extracts of the Chinese classics accurately translated which talk about first principles. Indeed, it would
even be desirable that all the classics be translated
together. But this not yet being done, one can only make
provisional judgments. Father Longobardi, S.J., Director of
the Mission of China -- following Father Ricci (who was the
first to go there) -- lived in China a great many years until
his death (being nearly 90 years of age), and he recorded,
in an incompletely published work, many passages of classical Chinese authors, but with the intent of refuting them.
Since this makes those passages much less suspect of having
been embroidered by him, I believe that what I might extract
from them in order to give a reasonable meaning to the authoritative dogmas of China would be more reliable, and less
subject to the suspicion of flattery. In addition, I will
appeal here and there to what Father Antoine de Sainte-Marie,
of the same opinion as Father Longobardi, has added to them.

§4   The first principle of the Chinese is called Li (2: 13),
that is Reason, or the foundation of all nature (5: 32), the
most universal reason and substance (11: 50); there is nothing
greater nor better than the Li (11: 53). This great and universal cause is pure, motionless, rarefied, without body or
shape, and can be comprehended only through the understanding.

From the <u>Li</u> qua <u>Li</u> emanate five virtues: piety, justice, religion, prudence and faith (11:49). [13]

§4a   Father de S. Marie, who also lived a long time in China and has also written against Chinese doctrine, says in his <u>Treatise on Some Important Points of the Mission of China</u> that their <u>Li</u> is the law which directs all things and is the intelligence which guides them (p. 62). It is the Law and universal Order, according to which Heaven and Earth have been formed (p. 65); the origin, source and principle of all which has been produced (p. 72). He notes [14] that the Japanese said to the missionaries that all things proceed in their very beginning from the power and virtue of the <u>Li</u>. As Father Luzena, [15] S.J., cited by Father de Sainte-Marie (p. 68) records in his History of the Arrival of Father Francois Xavier [16] to Japan (Book 8, Ch. 2), the <u>Li</u> is sufficient

---

13. Longobardi gives no transliterated Chinese terms here, and is not quoting from the <u>Compendium</u>. The reference must be to the <u>wu ch'ang</u> (五常) -- "5 constant [virtues]" -- of the Confucians: <u>jen</u> (仁), "benevolence," "human-heartedness"; <u>i</u> (義), "Righteousness, "justice"; <u>li</u> (禮), "ritual," "rites," "worship," "etiquette"; <u>chih</u> (智), "wisdom," "knowledge"; and <u>hsin</u> (信) "sincerity," trustworthy."

14. On p. 71.

15. Fr. Joao de Lucena S.J. (1548-1600), an early biographer of St. Francis Xavier.

16. One of the most famous missionaries to Asia, St. Francis Xavier S.J., (1506-1552), established missions in Goa, Japan and Macao. He planned a mission to China, but it never materialized. He was canonized in 1622.

unto itself so that the world has no need for another diety.
Thus, according to the Chinese, the Li is the sole cause
which always moves Heaven, throughout the centuries, in a
uniform motion. It gives stability to the earth; it endows
all species with the ability to reproduce their kind, this
virtue not being in the nature of the things themselves and
not depending at all upon them but consisting and residing
in this Li. It has dominion over all; it is present in all
things, governing and producing all as absolute master of
Heaven and Earth (p. 73). Father de Sainte-Marie adds:
see the Chinese texts in their Philosophy Kingli (I believe
it should read Singli),[17] Book 26, p. 8.[18]

§5   In the 14th section of his work (14: 74), Father Longobardi compiles the qualities which the Chinese attribute to
this first principle. They call it (par excellence) the
Being, the Substance, the Entity. According to them, this
substance is infinite, eternal, uncreated, incorruptible
and without beginning or end. It is not only the principle
of the physical basis of Heaven and Earth and other material

---

17.   The Compendium. See Introduction, pp. 30-31.

18.   Following this paragraph was a section struck out which reads:

      After all this, why not simply say that the Li is our God?
      That is, the ultimate, or if you wish, the primary ground
      of Existence and even of the possibility of things; the
      source of all good which is in things, the primary intelli-
      gence which was called by Anaxagoras and other ancient
      Greeks and Latins, NOUS, Mens.

things, but also the principle of the moral basis of virtues, customs and other spiritual things. It is invisible,
it is perfect in its being to the highest degree, and it
is itself all perfections.[19]

§6   The Chinese also call it the Supreme; or, as Longobardi says, they call it the Summary Unity because as in
the number series, unity is the basis, yet is not itself a
member.   Also, among substances, the essences of the universe, one of them is absolutely unitary, not at all capable
of divisibility as regards its being and is the principal
basis of all the essences which are and which can exist in
the world.   But it is also the aggregate of the most perfect
multiplicity because the Being of this principle contains
the essences of things as they are in their germinal state.[20]
We say as much when we teach that the ideas, the primitive

19. According to Leibniz, "perfection" refers to any attribute or essential property of a thing which makes it a "perfect" example of what
it is. Something is "perfect in its being" if it is wholly and completely itself, i.e., has all the properties or perfections necessary
to its essential being. God is Himself all perfections (by definition)
and, containing all these perfections in the highest degree, is the
cause of them in other beings.
20. Following the words "Longobardi says . . .," up to "germinal
state," Leibniz is quoting the former directly, except that all empha-
ses are Leibniz's, and he has interpolated the emphasized phrase "the
most perfect multiplicity." The expression "Summary Unity," which
Longobardi refers to frequently, is t'ai i (太 一), "Great One."

grounds, the prototypes of all essences, are all in God.
And conjoining supreme unity with the most perfect multiplicity, we say that God is: "One and all things, one
containing all; all things embraced in one; but formally,
all things as its perfection."[21]

§7   In the same section Father Longobardi mentions that
the Chinese say that the Li is the Grand Void, the immense
capacity (or Space), because this universal Essence contains all particular essences. But they also call it the
sovereign plenitude because it fills all and leaves nothing
empty. It is extended within and without the universe.
These matters (he says) are dealt with thoroughly in the
Chung-Jung (one of the books of Confucius) from Chapters
20 through 25.[22]   In the same way we explain the immensity
of God: He is everywhere and everything is in Him. So
also Father Lessius has said that God is the place of

---

21. Unum omnia, Unum continens omnia, omnia comprehensa in uno, sed
Unum formaliter, omni eminenter.
22. Chung Yung is about, but not written by, Confucius. The claim of
authorship comes from Leibniz himself, not from Longobardi. The expression t'ai hsü (太虛) -- "Great Void" or "Great Plenum" -- was
originally a Taoist and Buddhist term. It came into Confucian parlance
with Chang Tsai 張載 (1020-1077), who used the term to denote ch'i
in its uncondensed form, as pure ether, without form. While formless,
the t'ai hsü nevertheless existed, and Chang's usage of the term was
designed to combat the Buddhist view of non-existence.

things, and Mr. Guirike, inventor of the vacuum machine,
believes that space pertains to God.[23] In order to give
an appropriate sense to this, it is necessary to conceive
of space not as a substance which possesses parts upon
parts, but as the order of things insofar as they are considered existing together,[24] proceeding from the immensity
of God inasmuch as all things depend upon him at every
moment. This order of things among themselves arises from
their relationship to a common Principle.[25]

---

23. Leonard Lessius (1554-1623) was a Flemish Jesuit active in doc-
trinal disputes within the Church. Otto von Guericke of Magdeburg
(1602-1686) performed an experiment in 1654 involving the creation
of a vacuum by pumping the air out of hemispherical containers.
Leibniz mentions this experiment (as well as Torricelli's in 1643,
where he emptied the air out of a glass tube by means of mercury) in
his correspondence with Clarke (Fifth Paper, #34). Leibniz, like the
Aristotelians and the Cartesians, did not admit the existence of a
true void and often used their arguments to support his views. Ibid.
24. In his last years, Leibniz often used this same language to
describe the nature of space (e.g., Ibid., #29). Leibniz believed
that he had sufficiently demonstrated that space cannot be real or
absolute, but is purely ideal, i.e., the perceived mutual relations
of co-existing things. Space is "only an order of things, like time,
and in no sense an absolute being." (Ibid., Fourth Paper, Postscript;
Parkinson, p. 220.) For Leibniz's many arguments -- direct and indi-
rect -- against the reality of space, see the Leibniz-Clarke Correspondence, Third Paper, ##3-5; Fourth Paper, ##7-11 and Postscript;
Fifth Paper, ##27-29; 33-47.
25. According to Leibniz, God not only created all, but sustains and
governs through "pre-established harmony." See §14 and fn. 48.

§8 The Chinese also call their Li a globe or circle.[26] I

believe that this agrees with our way of speaking, since we

speak of God as being a sphere or a circle whose center is

everywhere and whose circumference is nowhere.[27] They call

it the Nature of things, which I believe corresponds to our

---

26. Represented by the Yin-Yang symbol ☯ , called t'ai-chi 太極 ,
the "Supreme Ultimate." This is a basic term in Neo-Confucianism, to
which Leibniz refers. The light part of the symbol represents yang, the
dark, yin (see Introduction, p. 20). For the Chinese, these forces are
complementary and not antagonistic, indicated in the symbol itself: each
side penetrates the other, and each contains an element of the other within it. Longobardi discusses the relationship of t'ai chi to yin and yang
at some length (e.g., 5:31, 32), and Ste. Marie does too; but Leibniz
makes no mention of yin and yang in the Discourse and does not discuss
t'ai-chi in detail.

27. Leibniz uses this same image for God in his Principles of Nature
and of Grace, Founded on Reason (1714), #13. Loemker says that "Leibniz
may have learned [of it] from Pascal, or from the German Rosicrucians
and theosophists." (II, 1203) More specifically, Leibniz's actual
source may well be Nicholas of Cusa who devotes many passages to expli-
cating this image. In turn Cusa, or perhaps even Leibniz himself, might
have learned of this image for God from the Hermetic tradition. In
their edition of Cusa's works, E. Hoffman and R. Klibansky quote a passage from "Hermes Trismegistus" written in language identical to that of
Leibniz's. "Deus est sphaera infinita, cuius centrum est ubique; circum-
ferentia nullibi." Liber XXIV philosophorum, prop. 2. Cited in Nicolaus
Cusanus: De Docte Ignorantia, p. 104, notes on lines 1-3. Also see
Wittkower, p. 28, n. 2. Leibniz often used notions and images of Cusa in
his writings, including the notion of each creature mirroring every other
as well as God, the latter "mirroring" being Cusa's explanation of God's
immanence as well as an excellent example of the Microcosm-Macrocosm mo-
del that Leibniz used. See fn. 136.

saying that God is the Natura Naturans.[28]   We say that Nature is wise; that she does all for an end and nothing in
vain.   The Chinese also attribute to it truth and goodness
as we attribute it to Being in our metaphysics.   But apparently for the Chinese, just as the Li is Being par excellence so it also possesses Truth and Goodness par excellence.
Father Longobardi adds that the author (I believe he means
Confucius, author of the Chung-Jung)[29] proves his statement
by referring to 18 passages from other, more ancient authors.

§8a   In conclusion: Father Longobardi notes that the
Chinese also attribute to the Li all manner of perfections,
so that there can be nothing more perfect.   It is sovereignly
spiritual and invisible; in short, so perfect that there is
nothing to add.   One has said it all.

§9   Consequently can we not say that the Li of the Chinese
is the sovereign substance which we revere under the name
of God?   But Father Longobardi objects to this (14: 78 ff.).
Let us see if his reasons for doing so are sufficient.   I
imagine (he says) that someone could believe that the

---

28. Natura naturans is a scholastic term used to distinguish the active, creative power of nature, viz., God, from natura naturata,
created nature of substance, viz., the world.
29. Longobardi's citation is ambiguous. See fn. 22.

Li [30] is our God because one ascribes to it those qualities and perfections which are appropriate only to God. However, do not let yourself be dazzled by these specious names under which a poisonous doctrine is hidden. For if you penetrate to the very heart of the matter, to its very root, you will see that this Li is nothing other than our prime Matter. The proof of this is that on one hand they ascribe to it grand perfections while on the other they ascribe to it grand imperfections as our philosophers do with respect to prime Matter. I have recorded the actual words of Father Longobardi and will examine them with care, for it appears that he is wide of the mark.

§10   I will first respond in general to the Father's comments: if the Chinese have themselves forgotten so much that they speak in a manner which appears so contradictory, one should not be assured thereby that the Li of the Chinese is prime matter rather than God. [31]   Initially, one should

---

30. All emphasized sentences are a direct quotation from Longobardi, except that after "Li," Longobardi has "or Tai-Kih," which Leibniz has omitted.

31. As Leibniz says below (§12), prime matter is purely passive, capable only of receiving motions or shapes from an active power (e.g., forms or entelechies) and is hence incapable of the active powers ascribed to the Li. Without being informed with a soul or entelechy or some sort of power of activity, matter is never a genuine or complete substance according to Leibniz and can be known only in abstraction from

suspend judgment and see which of the two opinions is the
more plausible and whether there is not a third one as well.
One should also see if they do not ascribe to the Li more
of the attributes of God than the attributes of prime matter and if the first of the two doctrines does not have more
in common with the rest of their doctrine. For my part, I
fear that the good Father Longobardi, already prejudiced
against Chinese doctrine, has himself been "dazzled" by the
writings of certain Mandarin Atheists, who have ridiculed
those who wish to draw consequences from the doctrines of
their ancestors in order to establish the Divinity, Providence and the rest of natural religion. One should no more
trust the obviously strained interpretation of such people
than one would trust those of an Atheist in Europe who would
try to demonstrate by passages pulled out of context, from
Solomon and other holy authors, that there is no reward or
punishment beyond this life.[32]   And if by misfortune
Atheism should prevail in Europe and become the doctrine of
the most learned -- as there was a time when Averroism almost prevailed among the philosophers of Italy -- then if
missionaries were sent to Europe by the sages of China and

---

it. Loemker, I, 560, n. 79. Secondary matter (see §23) refers to the
matter of individual bodies subject to the various laws of physics
(e.g., inertia, resistance, etc.).
32. Ecclesiastes 9:2-5.

they studied our ancient books, they would have reason to
oppose the wave of opinion of these most learned men and to
ridicule their ridicule.

§11   Father de Sainte-Marie (p. 84, 85), recounting the
great and good things the Chinese say of the Li, the Taikie
and the Xangti,[33] which are appropriate only to God on the
one hand, but which they deprive of all consciousness on the
other, believes that they thereby contradict one another.
But if this is the case, why do they not cling to the good
which they ascribe to it, refuting and rebutting that which
they say is bad and contradictory of the good? According
to the Chinese, the Li or the Taikie is the one par excellence, pure goodness without admixture, a being completely
simple and good, the principle which formed Heaven and
Earth; it is supreme truth and strength in itself, yet not
confined to itself; and in order to manifest itself, created all things. It is the source of purity, virtue and
charity. The creation of all things is its proper science,
and all perfections come from its essence and its nature.
This principle comprehends all the ways and the laws of

---

33. T'ai chi (see fn. 26) and Shang ti 上帝 , "Lord-on-high." This
latter term goes back to high antiquity; in its earliest use it probably
referred to the first ancestor of the ruling family. Many translators,
from Longobardi's time to the present, translate Shang ti as "God." See
also fn. 89.

reason (external as well as internal to itself), by which it disposes of all in its time without ever ceasing to act or create. It can be assumed that the Li, Taikie, or Xangti is an intelligent nature which sees all, knows all and can do all. Now the Chinese could not without contradiction attribute such great things to a nature which they believed to be without any capacities, without life, without consciousness, without intelligence and without wisdom.[34] But the Father responds that pagan philosophers have also advanced things which imply contradiction. I believe that the contradictions are indeed expressed in the language they use, in terminus terminantibus.[35] One can, however, attribute them to different sects. Or if they are within the same sect, one should seek a conciliation and do so in the most reasonable fashion.

§12 But turning to the details [of my objection to Longobardi's argument], I do not at all see how it could be possible for the Chinese to elicit from prime matter -- as our philosophers teach it in their schools, as purely passive, without order or form -- the origin of activity, of order and of all forms. I do not believe them to be so stupid or absurd. This scholastic notion of prime matter

34. See the conclusion of §16b.
35. I.e., "in the terms to be defined."

has no other perfections beyond that of Being, other than
that of receptivity, i.e., passive power. It has only the
capacity to receive all sorts of shapes, motions and forms.
However, it could never be the source of them. It is clear
as day that the active power, and the perception which regu-
lates this active power to operate in a determinate manner,
are not suited to it. Therefore, I believe that it is quite
inappropriate to equate the Li of the Chinese -- which is
Reason or Order -- with prime matter.

§13   During the time of the Scholastics, there was a certain David of Dinant[36] who held that God was the prime matter
of things. One could say the same of Spinoza who appeared
to hold that creatures are only modes of God.[37]   But prime

---

36. Little is known about this figure, except that he taught in Paris at
the beginning of the 13th century. He is known as a materialistic pan-
theist, but our knowledge of him is mostly from other sources. He held
a monistic view of reality where God, mind and matter were essentially
undifferentiated (i.e., possessed no essential forms). According to
Dinant, if God and matter have no form, they are being in potentiality
or prime matter. Thus, "The ultimate reality, which is at once God, mind,
and matter, is best described as matter." "David of Dinant," Encyclopedia
of Philosophy, vol. I, 306.

37.   In Book I, Definition of the Ethics, Spinoza says, "By mode I
understand the modifications of substance, . . ." Furthermore, Propo-
sition XIV of the same Book states, "Besides God no substance can be
nor can be conceived." Hence anything which is, is a mode of God.

matter in the sense of these authors is not a purely passive
thing, for it contains in itself the active principle. It
could be that some Chinese had similar ideas, but one cannot
thus simply accuse their whole school of such ideas.[38]   Among
us, one often says that the soul is part of God, divinae
particulae aurae.[39]   Such expressions require a charitable
interpretation. God has no parts at all and if one claims
that the soul is an emanation of God, one should not imagine
thereby that the soul is a portion which is detached from
Him and to which it must return as a drop of water to the
ocean. Such would render God divisible, whereas in fact the
soul is an immediate production of God. Some philosophers,
such as Julius Scaliger,[40] have held that forms are not at
all the result of matter, but the result of an efficient

---

38. The context here makes it difficult to tell whether Leibniz is referring to 1) all Chinese philosophers; or 2) the literati -- i.e.,
the Confucians; or 3) those syncretistic thinkers of the Ming-Ch'ing
times who were attempting to merge the "3 Schools" into one.
39. "A particle of the divine breath."
40. Julius Caesar Scaliger (1484-1558) was a student of the Aristotelian
Renaissance scholar Pietro Pomponazzi. He is confused at times with
his famous son, Joseph Justus Scaliger (1540-1609), a Greek and Roman
scholar.

cause; this was sustained by the Traducians.[41]   But one may
not say that the soul could have emanated from the substance
of God in such a way as to grant parts to God; therefore the
soul can only be produced from nothing.   Consequently if
some Chinese philosopher says that things are emanations of
the Li, one should not immediately accuse him of making Li
the material cause of things.

§14   I believe that one can take the passage from the
book entitled Chu-zu (Chap. 28 of the [Hsing-li] Philosophy,
p. 2) that Father Longobardi cites, in the above sense.
This author [Chu Hsi] says very wisely that the Spirits are
not merely air, but the force of air.   And if Confucius has
said to one of his disciples that the Spirits are only air,

---

41. Both Scaliger (see fn. 40) and the Traducians objected to the theory
that substantial forms and souls "were derived from the potency of matter, this being called Eduction." (Theodicy, #88) Scaliger and the
Traducians opposed this theory with one of Traduction, where souls are
propagated in a similar way to the procreation of the body, thus, in
effect, being transmitted by the parents to their children. Leibniz
himself inclines to such a theory in a modified form to explain the origin of human souls as well as organic bodies in general.

   This production [of human souls] is a kind of traduction,
   but more manageable than that kind which is commonly
   taught; it does not derive the soul from a soul, but
   only the animate from an animate, and it avoids the repeated miracles of a new creation, which would cause a
   new and pure soul to enter a body that must corrupt it.
   (Theodicy, #397; Allen, 166)

he meant animated air and was accommodating himself to the intellectual capacity of this disciple, scarcely capable of conceiving spiritual substances.[42] Thus for the Greeks and the Latins, Pneuma, Spiritus, signifies air; that is a subtle and penetrating matter in which created immaterial substances are in effect clothed.[43] The same author (book 28, p. 13) adds a little later that the Spirits are called Li. I judge that the word is ambiguous and is sometimes taken as Spirit par excellence, sometimes also as any spirit, for it may be the case that etymologically, it signifies reason or order.[44] The Chinese author, according to the translation which Father Longobardi gives us, proceeds as follows:

---

42. Here and elsewhere in the text Leibniz attributes to Confucius a pedagogy that geared the Master's teachings to the intellectual and spiritual development of his students. While there are many passages in the Lun Yü which show that Confucius did indeed evaluate the progress of his followers, there is little evidence to suggest, as Longobardi and Ste. Marie do, that he had an esoteric doctrine transmitted only to advanced initiates. Leibniz argues this point explicitly in §49.

43. See fn. 6.

44. The character 理 has two components: 玉 and 里 . The former is the term for jade, and the latter is the term for the Chinese mile (about 1/3 of a mile). 里 in turn is made up of the term for field 田 , and the term for earth 土 . Chinese etymologies suggest that the compound Li of which Leibniz speaks (理) originally referred to the venation in pieces of jade, and thus came to have the meaning of order, or pattern. See Karlgren (1), #978.

The Spirits are all from the same Li,[45] so that the Li is the substance and the universal Being of all things. I would imagine that he means to say that the Li is, so to speak, the quintessence, the very life, the power and principal being of things, since he has expressly distinguished the Li of the air from the matter of the air. It appears that here the Li does not signify prime spiritual substance but spiritual substance or entelechy[46] in general; that is

---

45. In quoting Longobardi here, Leibniz omits a phrase. In this section of the Religion Treatise Longobardi is discussing the different kinds of spirits in Chinese religion, and his statement begins: "These spirits, as well as others, called Li . . . ."

46. For Leibniz, every substance qua substance is such by virtue of an internal unifying active power or force. Leibniz uses the Aristotelian term ENTELECHEIA to denote this activity (as well as a synonym for substance itself, especially immaterial ones -- see §21), believing that he alone was faithful to its original sense, unlike later medieval commentators on Aristotle (see end of §38). Entelechy is used by Leibniz as a more inclusive term than soul, the latter usually being reserved for those substance or monads "whose perception is more distinct and is accompanied by memory." (Monadology, #19) Yet in other writings, such as the present text, he several times uses "entelechy" as synonymous with "soul" or "spirit" (see §21). Occasionally, if Leibniz wishes to stress the immaterial aspect of some entelechies, he adds the word "first" or "primitive" (see §19). In this sense, he is conforming to Aristotle's distinctive use of "first entelechy": (De Anima, II, 412a, 20-29) as the form or actuality of living, natural bodies. Directly below Leibniz pluralizes Li, which should cause discomfort to some sinologists. In his review of the Loosen-Vonessen German translation of the Discourse, Zempliner argues that these passages show that for Leibniz, li = monads (p. 228).

it signifies what is endowed with activity and perception or
orderly action as souls are. And since [Chu Hsi] adds, <u>that
things have no other difference among them than that of being
more or less coarse, more or less extended matter</u>,[47] he apparently wants to say, not that the <u>Li</u> or Spirits are material,
but that those things animated by spirits, and those conjoined to material less coarse and more extended, are more
perfect. It is easy to see that this author has not pene-
trated enough into this issue and that he has sought the
source of the diversity of Spirits in their bodies -- as has
been done by many of our own philosophers, who have not known
of pre-established harmony[48] -- but at least he has said nothing

---

47. Although Leibniz underlines here, he is paraphrasing Longobardi and
not quoting directly.

48. As in this context, Leibniz usually invoked the celebrated doctrine
of pre-established harmony in conjunction with the mind-body problem.
Leibniz sees the Chinese facing the same difficulty as the rationalists
(e.g., the Cartesians) of his day, namely, how to explain the interaction
of "immaterial qualities" and "material particles," or more specifically,
of a soul with its own body, given that each is a totally different substance with no common attributes. Since he has already rejected the alternative of strict materialism for the Chinese, and finds Descartes'
answer unintelligible, Leibniz believes:

> there remains only my hypothesis, that is to say, the <u>way
> of pre-established harmony</u> -- pre-established, that is, by
> a Divine anticipatory artifice, which so formed each of
> these substances from the beginning, that in merely fol-
> lowing its own laws, which it received with its being, it
> is yet in accord with the other, just as if they mutually
> influenced one another . . .

false. Thus his intention is not at all to make the Li's or
Spirits (and much less the Li absolutely or principally) material.[49] He is far from this since he has just distinguished
between air and the Spirits which animate it. Nor does he
say that the Li is the matter of things but seems to suggest
that the individual's Li's are more or less perfect emanations (according to their bodies) of the great Li. Consequently the differences of things are proportionate to the
subtlety and the extension of their matter, since their Li's
themselves correspond to them. In this he says nothing which
is not true.

§15   However, having provided explicit passages from the
Chinese classical authors which make the Li the source of
perfection, Father Longobardi cites none which show it to be
the formless prime matter of the Scholastics, which he claims

---

(New System, and Explanation of the New System; Parkinson, p. 131). Further, all substances (and not just an individual soul and its body) are
created and preformed with certain natural dispositions or propensities
(see §18), which they will actualize naturally in time and in keeping
with the pre-established harmony that God ordained from the beginning.
This perfectly timed and executed correlation of all substances not only
solves the mind-body problem for Leibniz, but also affords a satisfactory
explanation for causation without resorting to "influxes" or other invisible and unintelligible causal agencies.
49. Leibniz is here laying the groundwork for the argument he will de-
velop in §23.

to prove by reasoning; but his reasoning is not as clear as
the explicit [Chinese] passages. Here are his reasons (14;
79) which I find very weak: (1) He says that Li cannot subsist by itself and has need of primal air.[50] I do not know
if the Chinese say that explicitly. Perhaps they would say
that it cannot act by itself because it naturally acts in
things, since it produces things only by means of prime matter by which they apparently mean this primal air. Thus he
has only demonstrated thus far that the Li is not prime matter.

§16 His second reason is that according to the Chinese,
the Li, considered in itself, is inanimate, without life,
without design and without intelligence. Elsewhere the
Father records views which confirm this. The universal cause,
he says (5: 32), according to the Chinese scholars, has
neither life nor knowledge nor any other power; they say the
same of Heaven, where the Li manifests itself most clearly.
The father cites the Xu-King (11:54; one of the earliest of
Chinese works), Book I, p. 33, where it is said that Heaven,
which is the most significant thing of the world, neither

---

50. "Primal air" is ch'i 氣 . The French is primogene, meaning
"first generated or produced [air]." Elsewhere Leibniz uses protogene in
the same way.

sees, nor understands, nor hates, nor loves.[51] He also cites
the Chinese [Hsing-li] Philosophy, Book 26, pp. 16-17, where
it is said that Heaven and Earth have neither reason, will nor
deliberation. And Father de Sainte-Marie (p. 81), following
Father Ricci, cites the Lung-iu, Chapter 14, where in expli-
cating the Li as the Tao (order), Confucius says that it is
incapable of knowing man, but man is capable of knowing it.[52]
One must, however, have a very exact translation of this passage in order to see if Confucius speaks there of the first
principle, or whether he is not speaking of law or order in
abstracto as when one also says among us that the law knows no
one, that is, it has no regard for the individual before it.

---

51. The reference here must be to Shu Ching, Part II, Book II, 7, which
Leibniz also cites below (see fn. 58). Legge (vol. III, p. 74) translates
the passage so that it flatly contradicts Longobardi's: "Heaven hears and
sees as our people hear and see; Heaven brightly approves and displays its
terrors, as our people brightly approve and would awe . . . ." The thrust
of Confucian thought on this issue, however, is much better captured by
Karlgren's translation of the same passage: "Heaven's seeing and hearing
(proceed from) work through our people's hearing and seeing, Heaven's
(enlightenment) discernment and (fearsomeness) severity work through our
people's discernment and severity (sc. against bad rulers)." (See Karlgren (2), p. 9.) That is, the will of Heaven is expressed, and known,
through human deeds.

52. The reference is to Lun Yü 15:28, which reads jen neng hung tao, fei
tao hung jen 人能弘道非道弘人   . The term "hung" does not
mean "know," and the translation should read: "Men can enlarge Tao; Tao
cannot enlarge men."

§16a   In addition, I answer that if the classical Chinese
authors deny to the Li, or first principle, life, knowledge,
and power, they mean without doubt these things in human
form and as they exist among created beings.[53]   By life, they
would mean the animation of organs; by knowledge the knowledge which is acquired by reasoning or experience; and by
power they would mean the power such as that of a prince or
magistrate who governs his subjects only by awe and by hope.[54]

§16b   However, in ascribing to the Li the greatest perfections, they ascribe to it something more exalted than all
this, of which the life, knowledge and power of creatures are
only shadows or feeble imitations. It is somewhat like those
mystics -- among others Dionysius the Pseudo-Areopagite --
who have denied that God could be a Being, ens, ON, but have

---

53. Leibniz is alluding here to the via negativa or "negative way" (usually associated with mystical theology), which claims that since God is
infinite and transcendant, we cannot ascribe -- but indeed must explicitly
negate -- any predicates (e.g., life, knowledge, power) that are associated with finite, created beings. Thus God may only be described by
denying Him any characteristic that implies such finitude. Indeed, the
use of the word "infinite" is the best example of such an approach. See
also fn. 55 below.

54. Leibniz is referring back to Longobardi here, and the latter was
using, in this context, "life," "knowledge," and "power" as his own
terms, not as translations from the Chinese.

said at the same time that he could be greater than being, super-ens, HYPEROUSIA.[55]   Thus do I understand the Chinese, who say, according to Father de Sainte-Marie (p. 62), that the _Li_ is the law which governs, and the intelligence which leads, things; that it is, however, not itself intelligent, but through natural force, its operations are so well regulated and sure, that one could say that it is intelligent. In our way of speaking, where one must seek and deliberate in order to act properly, we would say that the _Li_ is more than intelligent; whereas for the Chinese it is infallible by its very nature.   As for Heaven and Earth, perhaps the author, in speaking of them, believed that they truly lack knowledge (which we believe too), although they are governed by knowledge, reason and order.

§17   The third argument [of Longobardi's] is that the _Li_ acts only contingently and not by will or deliberation.   From

---

55. Virtually nothing is known about Pseudo-Dionysius, as he is more often called, except that his writings were first cited in the 6th century and that he was clearly a devout Christian who had absorbed the traditions of late Neo-Platonism concerning the "negative way" of describing God (see fn. 53) even more strongly than the later mystics such as Nicholas of Cusa. Pseudo-Dionysius claims that one cannot even say that God "exists" or has "Being." Although the "Cause and Origin and Being and Life of all creatures (_The Divine Names_, I, 3) [God] "Itself exists not, for It is beyond all Being." (_Ibid._, I, 1.)

the Li (5 : 33), the primal air[56] is emitted naturally and contingently; equally naturally and contingently (34) the agi-
tated air produced heat, and (36) consequently the creation
of Heaven and Earth occurred purely contingently in a manner
quite natural, i.e., with neither deliberation nor design.
He also says (11 : 54) that Heaven and Earth act only by natural propensity, just as fire burns and stones fall. Further (14: 77) the Li is the natural law of Heaven and by its
operation all things are governed, according to weight and
measure, and conforming to their state; not, however, on the
basis of intelligence or reflection, but only by propensity
and natural order. The governance (17: 88) and the order of
things of this world stems naturally and necessarily from
the Li, following the connectedness of all things, and the
disposition of individual subjects, which we call destiny.
The same Father says (17: 90), I asked a celebrated man,
leader of a school with a great number of disciples, who
understood perfectly the doctrine of the three sects (that is,
the literati, the bonzes or the idolators, and the Tao-cu,
which the Europeans call sorcerers),[57] I asked him (I said) if

---

56. See fn. 50.

57. "Doctrine" is in the singular in both Longobardi and Leibniz, so the
reference may be to the syncretist movements. The parenthetical remark,
however, suggests the three schools separately: the Confucians, Buddhists
and Taoists respectively.

the King-on-high (<u>Xangti</u> the Lord of Heaven) had life and intelligence, if he knew the good and evil which men do, and
if he rewarded and punished them. The response of this
learned man is noteworthy. He responded that <u>the King-on-high</u>
<u>had none of this knowledge but acted as if he had</u>, thus con-
forming to what is said in the Xû-King, Book I, p. 35, that
Heaven neither sees nor understands nor loves nor hates, but
performs all these operations through the efforts of . . .
the people . . . with whom the <u>Li</u> is connected.[58]

§18   All these expressions of the Chinese have a rational
meaning. They say of Heaven what we say of the beasts,
namely that they act according to intelligence and as if they
possessed it, although they do not possess it at all because
they are directed by the supreme order or reason; which the
Chinese call <u>Li</u>. When they say that the primal air or matter
leaves the <u>Li</u> naturally and involuntarily, it could be they

---

58. The Longobardi text is ambiguous about who is quoting whom with respect to the <u>Shu Ching</u>. "For Heaven neither loving nor hating, etc.,"
see fn. 51. Leibniz, however, cites p. 35 for this quote, whereas he
earlier cites p. 33. The <u>Shu Ching</u> does make reference to Heaven 天
(<u>t'ien</u>) and Lord-on-high (<u>Shang ti</u>) in the Book following the last one
cited. The gist of the passage is that if the ruler is virtuous, and ap-
points only virtuous officials, the people will respond, showing that the
ruler has the support of the Lord-on-high, and that Heaven's mandate will
remain with him. Legge, vol. III, p. 79, and Karlgren (2), p. 11. Again,
in neither passage does <u>Li</u> occur.

believe that God has created matter necessarily. But one
could grant yet a better meaning to their words, explaining
them more fittingly: namely, that supreme Reason has been
brought to that which is the most rational. It is possible
they call the Li necessary, because it is determined and infallible; misusing the term "necessary" as many Europeans
do.[59] And they have excluded voluntary action because they
have understood by voluntary, an act of design and deliberation where at first one is uncertain and then one makes up
one's mind afterwards -- something which has no place in God.
Thus I believe that without doing violence to the ancient
doctrine of the Chinese, one can say that the Li has been
brought by the perfection of its nature to choose, from
several possibilities, the most appropriate; and that by this
means it has produced the Ki or matter[60] with dispositions
such that all the rest has come about by natural propensities, in the same way that Monsieur Descartes claims to bring
forth the present order of the world as a consequence of a
small number of initially generated assumptions. Thus the
Chinese, far from being blameworthy, merit praise for their
idea of things being created by their natural propensity and

---

59. This is not an example of Leibniz's best argumentative style. No
expression in ancient Chinese approximates the meaning of "necessary" as
used in Western philosophy and religion. Thus his "It is possible they
call the Li necessary, misusing the term, . . ." should be ignored.
60. See fn. 50.

and by a pre-established harmony.[61] But contingency [as
Longobardi uses it in his third argument] is not at all appropriate here and does not appear to be based in any way
on the words of the Chinese.

§19   The fourth objection of Father Longobardi is based on
a false supposition: he says that the Li is the subject of
all generation and of all corruption, taking on or discarding
various qualities or accidental forms. But there is nothing
in the passages that he quotes which says this of the Li, or
rule, or supreme Reason. They speak rather of the primal
air, or of matter, through which the Li creates the primitive
entelechies or the substantive operating qualities, which
form the constitutive principle of spirits.[62]

§20   His fifth objection is also based on a false or mistaken supposition: namely, that according to the Chinese all
things of the world are necessarily material and that there
is nothing truly spiritual. As proof of this he cites Books
26 and 34 of their [Hsing-li] Philosophy. He would have done
well, however, to give us the passages concerning this point.
But I believe (as I have already said)[63] that the Chinese

---

61. See fn. 48.
62. See fn. 46.
63. In §2.

recognize no distinct immaterial substance other than the Li
which has produced Matter. In this I believe they are correct and that the order of things brings it about that all
individual Spirits are always united to bodies and that the
soul, even after death, is never stripped of all organized
matter or of all informed air.[64]

§21   Father Longobardi relies heavily on the Chinese axiom
which says that all things are one. He mentions it expressly
(7: 41) and returns to it often.[65] Father de Sainte Marie also speaks of it (p. 72).[66] There is yet another passage
recorded by Father de Sainte Marie (p. 73) which shows that
there exists something more than material qualities. The
Sing-Li Philosophy, Book 26, p. 8, says that the directing
and procreating virtue is not found in the disposition of
things and does not depend on them but is composed of and
resides in the Li which has dominion over, governs, and produces all. Parmenides and Melissus spoke in the same way but
the sense which Aristotle gives them appears different from
the sense given to Parmenides by Plato.[67] Spinoza reduces all

---

64. See fn. 7.
65. And according to Longobardi, the Chinese learned this doctrine from
Zoroaster (7: 41).
66. Ste. Marie translates the saying Van-voe-ie-ti-Van-voe-ie-li (Wan
wu i ti, wan wu i li) 萬物一窗萬物一理   , without citation.
67. Leibniz introduces the references to these specific Greek philosophers
because Longobardi has done so in the same passage from which Leibniz has

to a single substance, of which all things are only modifications. It is not easy to explain how the Chinese understand it but I believe that nothing prevents according them
a rational interpretation. With respect to that which is
passive in them, all things are composed of the same prime
matter, which differs only by the forms which motion gives
it. Also, all things are active and possess Entelechies,
Spirits and Souls [68] only by virtue of the participation of
the Li, i.e., the same originative Spirit (God), which gives
them all their perfections. And matter itself is only a production of this same primary cause. Thus everything emanates
from it as from a central point. But it does not follow
from this that all things are different only by virtue of
accidental qualities: as, for example, the Epicureans and
other materialists believed, admitting only matter, figure
and movement, which would truly lead to the destruction of
immaterial substances, or Entelechies, Souls and Spirits.

---

just quoted. Aristotle interprets Parmenides as allowing for an efficient cause (i.e., of motion and attraction) as well as a material one,
thus diluting the strict interpretation of the Eleatics that all is one
and unchangeable. Metaphysics, Book I, Chap. 3, 984b 2-4; 30-31. Plato,
on the other hand, adheres to a stricter interpretation of Eleatic monism,
including Parmenides, which denies the existence of motion or genuine
plurality. Theatetus 180E; Parmenides, 137CD.
68. See fn. 46.

§22 The saying that all is one should be counterposed

with another, that the one is all, of which we have spoken

above in recounting the attributes of the Li.[69] It means

that God is everything by eminence, as the perfections of

effects are in their cause, and not formally, as if God

was the aggregate of all things. In the same way, all

things are one, but not formally as if they comprised one,

or as if this great One was their matter. Rather all things

are one by emanation, because they are the immediate effects

of Him; that is, He attends to them intimately and fully,

and expresses Himself in the perfections which He communi-

cates to them according to their degree of receptivity.[70]

And it is thus that one says Jovis omnia plena;[71] that He

fills all, that He is in all things and that also all things

---

69. I.e., in §4 through §8. Longobardi does not say "one is all"; Ste.
Marie and Leibniz use the expression.

70. The Stoics thought of reason as the creative fire (pneuma) or soul
residing in the individual as well as the world at large. God (or Zeus)
is often thought of as being the animating force or soul of the world,
the latter thus being a gigantic rational animal. In his correspondence
with Clarke (Fifth paper, #43), Leibniz makes the same point in criti-
cizing the notion that space is a property of God, thus in effect giving
Him divisible parts. "This God with parts will be very like the Stoic
God, who was the whole universe, considered as a divine animal." (Parkinson, p. 230). See also, "Letter to Hansch," Loemker, II, 996.

71. "Jupiter fills the universe," a phrase taken from Virgil's Eclogues,
III, 60.

are in Him. He is at the same time the center and the space because He is a circle of which the center is everywhere, as we have said above.[72] This sense of the axiom "that all is one" is all the more certain for the Chinese, since they attribute to the Li a perfect unity incapable of division -- according to the report of Father Longobardi noted above -- and what makes the Li incapable of division is that it can have no parts.[73]

§23 One could perhaps claim that in fact the Li cannot be equated with the prime Matter of our philosophers, but that one can conceive of it as the prime form, that is, as the Soul of the World, of which the individual souls would only be modifications. This would follow the opinions of several ancients, the opinions of the Averroists, and in a certain sense, even the opinions of Spinoza, for all of whom second-ary matters are only modifications of prime matter.[74] And consequently the supposed individual soul would be no more than those organs through which the Soul of the World oper-ates. This doctrine is not at all tenable, because each soul has its own individuality or self.[75] Individual matter is

---

72. See fn. 27.
73. See §6 and §14.
74. See fn. 31.
75. For Leibniz, prime matter itself is not genuinely substance (fn. 31), but gains its existence and identity as an individual substance only when

able to result from modifications of prime matter because prime matter has parts. But prime form or pure activity has no parts; thus secondary forms are not produced <u>from</u> the prime one, but <u>by</u> the prime one.[76] I do not want to deny that several Chinese may have fallen into this error, but it does not seem to me that the error can be found in the passages of their ancient writers.[77] Father Longobardi, who has spoken to many Mandarins trying to find passages contrary to our theology, would have cited some of them had he found them. Consequently I believe that one can claim [on behalf of the Chinese], without doing violence to their classical authors, that there are Spirits such as those of Man or genii which are of different substances than the <u>Li</u>, although they ema-nate from it.

---

it is informed with a form or soul. Hence for Leibniz, as for many Scholastics, individual identity is based on the particular form of a substance, not its individual or secondary matter, which is simply a modification of prime matter.

76. See fn. 49. Translators' emphasis.

77. Among those whom Leibniz believed fell "into this error" was proba-bly Chu Hsi, cited on this point in §14. The error will not be found in the "ancient writers" -- i.e., in the classical texts -- because dis-cussions about primary and secondary matter do not occur there.

[II.   Chinese Opinion Concerning the Productions of God or
Prime Matter, and Spirits]

§24   Having spoken enough concerning the Li, let us turn
to what it produces, following what Father Longobardi tells
us from the Chinese authors.   From the Li issues the air
(5: 39), the primitive air (11: 49), or the primogeneous (or
protogeneous) air (14: 79).   He calls this primitive air Ki
(10: 48 and 11: 56/57); it is the instrument of the Li
(11: 50).   The operations of the Spirits pertain ultimately
to the Li, instrumentally to the Ki, and formally to the
Spirits (11: 56).   It seems that this Ki, or this primitive
air, truly corresponds to Matter, just as it corresponds to
the instrument of the first principle which moves matter;
just as an artisan moves his instrument, producing things.
This Ki is called air, and for us could be called Aether
because matter in its original form is completely fluid,
without bonds or solidarity, without any interstices and
without limits which could distinguish parts of it one from
the other.   In sum, this matter (Ki) is the most subtle one
can imagine.

§24a   Now Father Longobardi expressly states that this Ki
is a production of the Li.   But he also says (5: 33) that
from the Li the primal air has naturally issued and (11:
56) although the Li performs no operations itself, it

commences to do so after having produced its Ki, that is,
its primitive Air. Either we must overlook the inconsis-
tency here, or admit that the good Father has made a mistake. How can one say that the Li does nothing itself,
without the Ki, if it produces the Ki? Can one create
without acting? And since the Ki is only the instrument,
isn't it necessary to say that its virtue or its principal
efficient cause is in the Li? In consequence of this production of prime Matter by the primary principle, or primitive Form, by pure Activity, by the operation of God,
Chinese philosophy more closely approaches Christian theology
than the philosophy of the ancient Greeks who considered
matter as coeval with God, a principle which produces nothing but only informs it. Admittedly, it appears that the
Chinese believed that the Li first and always produced its
Ki and that therefore one is as eternal as the other. But
there should be nothing surprising about this since they
were apparently ignorant of the one Revelation which can
explain to us the beginning of the universe -- St. Thomas
[Aquinas] and other great doctors having claimed that this
dogma could not be demonstrated by reason alone. However,
although the ancient Chinese expressly state that the Ki
never perishes, they do not explicitly state that it has no

beginning.[78] And there are those who believe that because the beginnings of the Chinese empire occurred during the time of the Patriarchs, they could have learned about the creation of the world from them.[79]

§25 It seems that after the Li and Ki comes the Taikie, but Father Longobardi has not written enough about the latter to give us a distinct idea of it.[80] One could almost say that the Taikie is nothing other than the Li working on the Ki: "The Spirit of the Lord who is borne upon the waters,"[81] taking the sovereign spirit for the Li,

---

78. Like li, ch'i is not used in a metaphysical sense in classical Confucianism, guaranteeing the truth of Leibniz's ". . . they do not explicitly state . . . ."

79. Prominent among those who so believed was Bouvet, who communicated this view to Leibniz in some detail in his letter of 4 November 1701. After referring to Fu Hsi as "the prince of all the philosophers," Bouvet went on to add that such a description was not an "atrocious offense against Europe," because Fu Hsi was not Chinese, but either Zoroaster, Hermes Trismegistus, or Enoch. Leibniz repeats this idea of the Patriarchs visiting China in §32 and §37. He also referred to it in other correspondence, cited by Merkel, pp. 84-85. Longobardi held a similar view (see fn. 65), and Ste. Marie suggests in the Mission Treatise (p. 21) that the Chinese are descendants of Noah.

80. Longobardi did discuss t'ai chi in some detail; Section 13 is devoted to it. See also fns. 26 and 33.

81. A slight paraphrase of the Latin vulgate edition of the Bible, Genesis 1: 2, Spiritus domini qui ferebatur super aquas.

and the waters for the primary fluid -- i.e., primal air or
Ki or prime matter. Thus the Li and Taikie would not be
different things but one and the same thing considered under
different predicates. The Father says (5: 33) that the Li
becomes an infinite globe (this is doubtlessly metaphorical)
which they name the Taikie -- that which has attained the
ultimate degree of perfection and consummation -- because
it operates effectively and exercises its virtue in the production of things, and gives them that ability which includes pre-established order in virtue of which everything
proceeds thereafter by its own natural propensity. Consequently, after creating natural objects God needs only
thereafter to proceed in his ordinary course.[82] This is why
it seems to me that the Father is somewhat confused (10: 47)
by confounding the Ki with the Taikie and saying that the
Taikie is the primal air.

§25a   Perhaps some Chinese assume that a primitive com-
posite has resulted from the primitive form, or Li, and
from the primitive matter or Ki; a substance of which the
Li is the soul and the Ki its matter. They could comprehend this substance under the name of Taikie, and the entire
world would thus be conceived of as an animal, life universal, supreme spirit, a grand personage; the Stoics speak

---

82. See fn. 48.

of the world in this fashion. Among the parts of this grand
and total animal would be the individual animals just as for
us animalcule enter into the composition of the bodies of
large animals. But since one does not find this error explicitly in the ancient Chinese authors, it should never be
attributed to them, all the more so since they have conceived
of matter as a production of God. God will not combine
substance with matter, and thus the world will not be an
animated being, but rather God will be an intelligentia
supramundana; and matter, being only an effect of His, will
never be coeval with Him. When Father Longobardi (11: 49)
says that the Taikie contains within itself the Li and the
primal air or Ki, one should not understand this to mean
that it is composed of them but simply that it contains them,
as conclusions are contained in their assumptions, because
the Taikie is the Li operating on the Ki and thus the Ki is
assumed.

§26   One may also attribute to the Taikie the attributes
of the Li. It is said (11: 53) that all the spirits issue
from the Taikie, that the Xangti is the son of the Taikie --
as a modern Mandarin said -- although one could perhaps be
sustained by the ancients in supporting the view that the
Xangti is also nothing other than the Li or Taikie conceived
as the governing principle of the universe, that is, Heaven;
as I will shortly demonstrate. Longobardi says (11: 54) that

the Spirits are the same Li or the same Taikie, applied to
different subjects, such as to Heaven, to Earth and to the
Mountains. The latter point is not in accord with what
the Mandarin said, however, for if the Xangti or the Spirit
of Heaven, is the son of the Taikie, it is not identical
with it. But sufficient to say here that the Taikie is
equated with the Li; we will see below what can be said of
the Xangti. Father Longobardi expresses the title of his
13th section in these terms, viz., that all the Gods of the
Chinese, or all the Spirits to which they attribute the
governance of things, reduce themselves to only one, which
is the Li or Taikie. Though it would be better do do so, I
am not going to examine this notion at present, but simply
note that [even for Longobardi] the Li and Taikie can be
taken for the same thing. He says, in this section (13: 68),
that the Li is the "cause of understanding and the guiding
norm of all nature";[83] immediately following, he says that the
Taikie is "nature's womb, containing in itself, potentially,
all possible things."[84] But he also states the latter of the
Li in 14: 75 and consequently he is certain (13: 68) that the
difference between the Li and the Taikie is only a formality
in that the Li denotes an absolute Being, while the Taikie

---

83. This and the following sentence which Leibniz quotes were written in
Latin by Longobardi: Mentis ratio et totius naturae regula directrix.
84. Sinus naturae continens in se virtualiter omnia possibilia.

denotes a Being with respect to things of which it is the root and origin. He cites Book 26 of the Chinese Philosophy, page 8, where it is said that causes act incessantly because the Li or the Taikie is within, governing them and directing them. And in Book One of the same text, page 31, it says that the Li (Reason) has dominion over the things of the world and consequently they lack nothing. Book 36, page 9 states that the Taikie is the cause of the beginning and the end of this world[85] and after a world is ended it produces another (5: 36) -- after the revolution of the great year called Ta Sui[86] (4: 32) -- but that it itself never ends. This proves that the Taikie is not the world. Finally, according to St. Marie (p. 69), the Chinese recognize nothing greater nor grander than the Li or the Taikie. They also [according to Longobardi] say that all things are the same Taikie. I believe this is not to be understood as if things are parts or modifications of the Taikie, because their absolute realities or perfections are emanations of it. But, just as we still often speak in a figurative way as if souls were particles of divinity, it should not then be

---

85. Longobardi's text reads "production and destruction" rather than "beginning and end."

86. Ta sui 大岁 , "Great year." The term denotes different time periods -- weeks, months, etc. -- and is also a name for the planet Jupiter. Thus the time period alluded to here is probably 12 years. Leibniz's citation should read 5: 32 instead of 4: 32.

surprising if the Chinese speak of them sometimes in the same manner. And it is in this sense that the Chinese Philosophy says in Book 26, page 1, that the Li is one, but that its parts are several. For to speak properly, a thing composed of parts is never truly One. It is unitary only by external denomination, as one pile of sand or one army. Thus the first principle does not have any parts -- as other passages already cited have shown.

§27   Father de Sainte Marie records passages (p. 64) from the Chinese where they seem to make up a word Li-Taikie. This word signifies (p. 69), according to Confucius (in the Chung-Jung, one of the four Books) substantial truth, Law, the principle and end of all things;[87] there is nothing which does not receive from it its effective and true being, without the essence of any of these things having a single atom of imperfection. It is somewhat like (the Father adds) what we read in Genesis [1:31]: God saw all that he had made and all was good. However, he then (p. 107/108) cites

---

87. This sentence follows Leibniz's text, but Ste. Marie does not imply that the Chinese "made up" a word for li/t'ai-chi in the Chung Yung. Again, li does not occur in this classical text; rather does the philosophically significant term tao 道 -- "Way" -- occur, and the later Neo-Confucian philosophers interpreted tao as signifying li in the ancient writings. Ste. Marie says that for him, the two expressions have the same meaning.

a passage from Lactantius concerning the first principle,
where this author, after having cited the ancient poets and
philosophers, says that all these opinions, although uncertain, establish providence under the names of Nature,
Heaven, Reason, Spirit, Fate, Divine Law, which all amount
to what we call God.[88] Father de Sainte Marie then adds
that the Chinese recognize only a material principle
divided into small parts. In this it seems to me that the
good Father is being misled by a strange prejudice which
comes to him not from classical authors but from the dis-
courses of some modern impious ones who, in China as elsewhere, see themselves as skeptics in order to set themselves
above the people.

§28 What the Chinese speak of as the most magnificent
after the Li or the Taikie is the Xangti, that is, the
King-on-high, or rather the Spirit which governs Heaven.
Having come to China and remaining there for some time,
Father Ricci believed that one could take this Xangti to
mean the Lord of Heaven and Earth; in a word our God, Whom
he also called Tien-chu,[89] the Lord of Heaven. In China, it

---

88. The Divine Institutes, Book I, Ch. 5.
89. T'ien-chu 天主 , "Heaven's Lord." This was Ricci's term for
"God," although he was willing to allow the ancient Chinese terms t'ien
and Shang ti to be translated in the same way. After the conclusion of
the Rites Controversy -- in which these terms were an issue -- only
T'ien-chu could be used by the Catholic missionary translators for "God."

is by this last term that one usually refers to the God of
the Christians. Fathers Longobardi, S. Marie and others
who do not sanction calling God Xangti are satisfied with
the name Tien-chu, although in effect the two terms signify almost the same thing in Chinese -- keeping in mind the
force of the terms "King-on-high" and "Lord of Heaven."
The main question is, whether the Xangti is an eternal
Substance or a mere creature for the Chinese. Father
Longobardi admits (2: 13) that the text (from the original
books) seems to say that there is a royal sovereign named
Xangti who lives in the palace of Heaven from which he
governs the world, rewards the good and punishes the wicked.
But on the same page, the Father presents the views of
other ancient interpreters who attribute these same qualities to Heaven, or to the universal substance called Li.
But far from being detrimental to those who give the name
of Xangti to our God, the term serves them marvelously.
For the Li is eternal and endowed with all possible perfections; in a word one can take it for our God, as I have
shown above. Thus if the Xangti and the Li are the same
thing,[90] one has every reason to give to God the name of
Xangti. And Father Ricci was not wrong to claim (Longobardi 16: 84) that the ancient philosophers of China recognized and honored a supreme being called Xangti, King-on-high,

---

90. This is Longobardi's claim.

as well as subordinate Spirits -- his ministers -- and that in this way, they had a knowledge of the true God.[91]

§29   The Chinese say yet other great and good things of Heaven, of the Spirit of Heaven, of the order of Heaven, all of which are most fittingly said of the true God. For example, they say (17: 99) the order of Heaven is the being of sovereign goodness which is imperceptible. And they call the Li (14: 77) the natural order of Heaven, insofar as all things are governed by weight and measure and con- form to their condition through the operation of the Li. This order of Heaven is called Tien-tao,[92] and according to Father de Sainte Marie (p. 69), Confucius in the Chung-Jung says that the Tien-tao is the same as the Li, the deter- minate order of Heaven in its course and its natural operations.[93] Consequently, according to the account of Father Longobardi (15: 81), the universal or primitive sub- stance qua the state it possesses in Heaven is called Li

---

91. Bouvet went further; according to him, the ancient Chinese, through the Patriarchs, had a knowledge not only of the true God, but of His triune nature as well. (Letter of 4 November 1701.)
92. T'ien-tao 天道 , "Heaven's Way."
93. Again, Leibniz appears to have misread Ste. Marie's text here, which reads: "Confucius, in the same place, speaking of the T'ien-tao, which is the same as the Li . . . ." Ste. Marie thus makes the two Chinese terms synonymous, but does not ascribe this view to Confucius. See also fn. 87.

(that is to say, order or reason). And the Li (14: 76) is
called an object in Heaven because the first principle, although it is present in all objects of the world is itself
primarily in Heaven -- which is the most excellent object
of the universe -- where its efficacy is most apparent. And
in Book 2, Chapter 5 of the Lun-Ju,[94] it is said of the Li
that this principle is of an incomparable essense and that
this principle is of an incomparable essence and that there
is nothing equal to it. So too the same praises are given
to Heaven, and therefore these praises can be reasonably
understood as being given not to matter, but to the Spirit
of Heaven or the King-on-high. So must Father de Sainte
Marie be understood when he says (p. 13) that the absolute
and supreme divinity of the Chinese literati is Heaven.[95]

§30   Here is how Father de Sainte Marie quotes a Chinese
doctor in speaking of the Xangti (p. 74): "Our Chinese

---

94. Because li does not occur in the Lun Yü, it is difficult to ascertain
what Leibniz and Longobardi are citing. Lun Yü 2: 5 discusses rituals,
the Chinese term for which is li 禮 , homophonous with li 理 , "Principle." The homonymy might have confused Longobardi, Ste. Marie, and/or
Leibniz, but it would not have confused any literate Chinese. Moreover,
there is no passage in the Lun Yü which treats of the "incomparable"
nature of the other terms with which li was often equated, except possibly
for 8: 19. Mungello suggests (Ch. 5) that it is a reference to 5: 12,
wherein it is said that one of the things Confucius refused to discuss
was "Heaven's Way," -- i.e., T'ien-tao.
95. Ste. Marie then goes on to describe Confucius as the Chinese Minerva.

philosophers, examining with great care the nature of Heaven and Earth and all things of the world, recognized that they were all good and that the Li was capable of containing them all, without exception, and that from the grandest to the smallest they possessed the same nature and the same substance, from which we conclude that the Lord or God Xangti is present in each thing, with which it is really one. For this reason, we should preach to men and exhort them to flee from vice which would dishonor and soil the perfections of the Xangti; to follow his justice, otherwise this would offend sovereign reason and supreme justice; and not to injure any beings because this would outrage the Lord Xangti, soul of all created things." This passage shows that according to its author, the Xangti is the universal substance, sovereignly perfect -- ultimately the same as the Li. One cannot sanction, however, the statements of this scholar (apparently modern) who would make the Xangti into the soul of things as if it were of their essence.

§31   The ancient sages of China, believing that the people have a need for objects in their cult which strike their imagination, did not want to propose to the public the reverence of the Li or of the Taikie, but rather the adoration of the Xangti, of the Spirit of Heaven, meaning by this name the Li or the Taikie itself, which manifests its power

principally [in Heaven].[96] At times the Hebrews also attribute to Heaven that which pertains to God -- as for example
in the Book of Maccabees[97] -- and they have considered God
the Lord of Heaven; for this reason, they were called
Coelicolae ["heaven-worshippers"] by the Romans: qui/Nil
praeter nubes, et coeli numen adorant.[98] Further,
Aristophanes, wanting to make Socrates odious and ridiculous
in the eyes of the Athenians, makes the people believe that,
contemptuous of the Gods of the land, [Socrates] reveres
Heaven or the clouds (which the ignorant confound);[99] this

---

96. This is a particularly obscure passage, which does not seem to make
sense without the interpolated phrase. Even with it, the translation
is tentative.

97. God is referred to as "Heaven" (OURANÓS) often in the Book of
Maccabees. For example: I, 3: 19, 4: 10, 24, 40, 55; 9: 46; 12: 15;
16: 3; also in II Maccabees: 7: 11; 9: 20. He is also called "Sovereign in Heaven" or "Sovereign of the Heavens."

98. The quote is from Juvenal's Satires, V, 14, 97: "They worship
nought but the clouds and a god of Heaven." There is no evidence that
the Romans referred to the Jews as Coelicolae. The verb colere has two
meanings: "to dwell (inhabit)," and "to worship." In the former sense,
the Romans used Coelicolae to refer to their own gods: "Heaven-dwellers."
(The editors are grateful to Mr. John Tagliabue for the information in
this footnote.)

99. ". . . il adoroit le Ciel, ou les nuages, ce que les ignorans con-
fondoient, . . ." Given the plot of The Clouds, and the thrust of
Aristophanes' attack on Socrates therein, the text should read "which
confound the ignorant." But the French phrase underlined above is clearly
to be translated as "which the ignorant confound."

can be seen in his comedy The Clouds. It is for this reason
Father de Sainte Marie says (p. 72), that the Chinese philosophers, ancient and modern, revere the visible Heaven and
sacrifice to it, under the name of King-on-high, Xangti,
because the dominant and visible quality of the Li is in-
comprehensible to the common people. But it would be better
to say that the Xangti, or that which the Chinese revere
principally, is the Li which governs Heaven, rather than
say that it is the material Heaven itself. Further on
(pp. 77/78), Father de Sainte Marie almost says the same
thing himself, the thrust of which is that the Chinese no
less than the Japanese (instructed doubtlessly by the
Chinese) recognize no other God than a first principle (he
adds, without foundation, material); that they call him the
supreme king, Xangti, in his capacity as having dominion
over Heaven; that Heaven is his Palace; that there on high
he leads and governs all and spreads his influence. They
sacrifice to this visible Heaven (or rather to its King) and
revere in profound silence that Li which they do not name
because of the ignorance or the vulgarity of the people who
would not understand the nature of the Li. What we call the
light of reason in man, they call commandment and law of
Heaven. What we call the inner satisfaction of obeying
justice and our fear of acting contrary to it, all this is
called by the Chinese (and by us as well) inspirations sent
by the Xangti (that is, by the true God). To offend Heaven

is to act against reason, to ask pardon of Heaven is to re-
form oneself and to make a sincere return in word and deed
in the submission one owes to this very law of reason. For
me, I find all this quite excellent and quite in accord with
natural theology. Far from finding any distorted understanding here, I believe that it is only by strained interpretations and by interpolations that one could find anything
to criticize on this point. It is pure Christianity, insofar as it renews the natural law inscribed in our hearts --
except for what revelation and grace add to it to improve
our nature.

§32   Regarding the Spirit which governs Heaven as the true
God, and taking it for the Li itself -- that is, for order
or for sovereign reason -- these ancient sages of China were
more nearly accurate than they realized. This is shown by
the discoveries of the astronomers that Heaven is the whole
known universe and our earth is only one of its subaltern
orbs; one can say that there are as many world systems as
there are fixed or principal stars, ours being the system
of the sun, which is only one of these stars. Thus the governor or Lord of Heaven is the Lord of the Universe. Since,
however, the Chinese have been fortunate enough to come by
this wisdom without sufficient warrant for it, it may be that
they learned part of it from the tradition of the Patriarchs.[100]

100. See fn. 79.

§33　Let us now see what Father Longobardi offers in con-
trast on this point. He says (2: 18) that according to
Chinese scholars, the Xangti is Heaven itself or rather the
virtue and the power of Heaven. But to say that the Xangti
is the material Heaven is implausible. As for its being the
virtue and power of Heaven, it could be nothing other than
the virtue and power of the entire universe, since Heaven
comprises all that we know of the universe. The idea of
some kind of individual soul for Heaven, which would be the
Xangti, is very unlikely, the expanse of Heaven being so
immense. It would make more sense to attribute a soul to
each system, or rather to each star, as the Chinese attribute one to the earth. The praises given to the Spirit of
Heaven, or to the Order of Heaven, would not be suitable to
an individual soul; they are appropriate only to the Li.
Thus (11: 52) if Ching Cheu, a classical author,[101] has said
that the Xangti is the same thing as Heaven, one can take
this expression as figurative or as less than exact, just
as we often use "Heaven" to denote the Lord in Heaven. It
may also be that this author considered Heaven as a person
of which the soul is the Li, and of which the body is the

---

101. Longobardi gives no sources here, and because he is not consistent
in his method of transliteration it is not possible to identify "Ching
Cheu," which does not occur elsewhere in the Religion Treatise. It is
probably the name of a Neo-Confucian commentator on the classics.

celestial material; and consequently he would have regarded
Heaven as the Stoics regarded this world. But until such
time as one can better examine this passage, it is more
plausible to think that he spoke figuratively (as is still
customarily done in Europe) in speaking of Heaven as God.

§34   According to Father de S. Marie (p. 57), ancient
Chinese writings contain the following anecdotes: the
Emperor Vuen-Wang[102] persevered all his life to be humble
and to hide the splendor of his majesty, to rectify himself
and to abase himself before this Lord and King-on-high,
Xangti. The Emperor named Hia Xi,[103] when he reproached himself for a wicked action, trembled in fear and respect before the Xangti and had the habit of saying that this fear
and respect restrained him so that he dared not commit a sin
against true reason. In ancient times the Emperor himself
cultivated the earth on which the seed offered to the sovereign

---

102. One of the transliterations for King Wen 文王 , founder of the
Chou Dynasty (1122-256 B.C.).

103. Ste. Marie (p. 57) provides no source for the anecdote of "Hia Xi,"
who is unknown. In the Loosen-Vonessen translation it is plausibly
suggested (p. 147) that the reference may be to the Shu Ching chapter in
which T'ang, founder of the Shang Dynasty says: "The Hsia sovereigns
[Hsia shih 夏氏] have offended; and because I fear Shang ti, I dare
not let them go unpunished." (Translation modified from Legge, vol. III,
p. 174.) If this suggestion is correct, however, then Ste. Marie (and
thus Leibniz) have attributed the lauded qualities to the wrong person.

King and Lord Xangti was sown. Further (p. 59), a King of
China asked Confucius if one should pray to the tutelary
god of fire or the more inferior one of the hearth. Confucius answered him that if one had given offense to Heaven
-- that is to the Lord of Heaven -- it is from him alone
that one should ask pardon.[104] This seems to show that Confucius, like Plato, believed in the unity of God but
accommodated himself to popular prejudices.[105]

§34a   Father Longobardi himself recounts (17: 90) the con-
versation which he had with a Chinese doctor, who told him
that the King-on-high or Xangti[106] was the same as Heaven,

---

104. Ste. Marie provides no source here, but the reference must be to
Lun Yü 3: 13. Only the term t'ien "Heaven," occurs therein, however;
Ste. Marie equates it with Shang ti ("Lord-on-high"), and Leibniz has
altered the equation to "Lord of Heaven."

105. Although most scholars believe, on both theological and etymologi-
cal grounds, that Plato was not a monotheist, there is nevertheless the
statement by Plato himself in Epistle XIII which shows that he could
make the distinction between "God" and "gods" if necessary. In writing
to Dionysius, Plato says:

> You no doubt recall the sign that distinguishes the letters
> I write that are seriously intended from those that are
> not . . . . Those that are seriously meant begin with
> "God"; those less seriously with "gods." Morrow, Plato's
> Epistles, p. 268.

Leibniz was clearly aware of these letters of Plato. For further details, see Riley, p. 209.

106. Neither Longobardi nor the Chinese doctor say "Xangti"; Leibniz
has added the phrase.

Li, Taikie, Iven-Ki [107] (the author does not explain this term),
the Tien-Xing [108] (or genii, p. 19), the Tien-Ming [109] (virtue
sent from Heaven), the Nan-lin [110] (virtue of the earth).
The same doctor also said that the Xangti of the literati
sect was the Spirit or the God which the Bonzes venerated
under the name of Foe [111] and the Tao-cu under the name of
Jo-Hoang. [112] Another has said (17: 87) that our heart (that
is what operates within us) is the same thing as the Xangti
and Tien-Cheu, for the Chinese say that the heart is the
Chu Zay [113] (or director) of man, regulating all his physical

---

107. Probably Yüan-ch'i 元氣 , "primal fluid." This term is first found
in the Huai Nan Tzu 淮南子 , an early metaphysical text of the Former Han Dynasty, written ca. 130 B.C. This work is not a part of the
Confucian classical corpus, but was widely read.

108. There are four possibilities here: 1) The term is T'ien-shen 天
神 , "Heavenly spirits"; 2) Being equated with li and T'ai-chi, however,
the term could be T'ien-hsing 天行 , "Heaven's conduct," or "Heaven's
path"; or it could be 3) T'ien-hsing 天性 , "Heaven's nature." The
last possibility would be 4) the Taoist term T'ien-hsien 天仙 ,
"Heavenly Immortals," suggested by Leibniz's parenthetical remark. See
also fn. 117.

109. T'ien-ming 天命 , "Heaven's mandate."

110. It is not clear what "Nan-lin" refers to; it is not a common Chinese
compound. Longobardi translates it as "Husband of the earth," which
Leibniz has altered.

111. Fo 佛 , i.e., the Buddha.

112. Yü-huang 玉皇 , the Jade Emperor, highest Taoist deity.

113. Chu-tsai 主宰 , "Supreme ruler."

and moral actions (15: 81). This shows how some Chinese often speak vaguely and confusedly under the pretext that all is one, and that one should not always take them literally. To be able to speak clearly of their dogmas, it is safest to consider the reason and the harmony of their doctrines, rather than individual utterances.

§35   Father Longobardi also recounts the discourse of Chinese Mandarins who told him that the Xangti and the Tien-Cheu, the King-on-high or Lord of Heaven, is only a production of the Taikie and will end like other creatures while the Taikie itself endures (11: 53); that the King-on-high or Spirit of Heaven will cease with Heaven (17: 89); and that if our God or our Tien-Cheu (Lord of Heaven) were the same as the Xangti, He would cease to exist as well (17: 87, 89). But the good Father produces no passage from the ancients which says as much.[114]   On the contrary, it would seem that the ancients wanted to revere the Li in the Xangti. These then are only the ideas of moderns, who try to substitute simple material substances for all spiritual substances, much as the Cartesians do with the souls of beasts,[115] and as some

---

114. Because the "ancients" didn't discuss the topic. Longobardi is not citing the classics, but his Chinese contemporary here.
115. As noted above (fns. 46, 48), Leibniz saw any substance qua substance as possessing some sort of soul or "spirit" (entelechy). On the other hand, Descartes and his followers, as strict dualists, thought of

ancients in the _Phaedo_ insisted, namely, that the soul is
nothing other than a harmony, or a congeries of material
dispositions, or a mechanical structure.[116] This tends only
to destroy religion (as if it were only a political invention) in order to hold the people in check, which is just
what a Chinese doctor said to Longobardi -- the same doctor
whose discourse, noted earlier, confounded different things
on the basis of a poor understanding of the notion that all
is one (17: 92).

§36   As taken absolutely, the Universal Spirit is called
_Li_ or Order; as operative in Creatures it is called _Taikie_
or that which consummates creation and establishes things;
as governing Heaven, the principle creation is called
Xangti, or King-on-High or _Tien-Chu_, Lord of Heaven.
Having established this, I want now to turn to the genii or
individual, subaltern Spirits. In general, they are called

---

beasts or brutes as as having no soul or spiritual qualities and therefore no consciousness at all. Animals for Descartes, are finely tuned
machines or automata (he likens them to watches; _The Passions of the
Soul_ Articles VII, XVI), made up only of matter set in motion by the
mechanical beat of the heart (_Discourse on Method_, V).
116. Simmias elaborates the theory that the soul is nothing but an
attunement (_HARMONIA_) of certain material elements of the body. _Phaedo_,
85B-86D. Cebes follows with another materialist argument against the
absolute immortality and indestructibility of the soul, claiming that
the latter may still "wear out" after many incarnations. _Ibid_, 87B-88C.

Tien Xin (Longobardi, Preface, p. 6) or simply Xin (8: 44),
or rather Kuei-Xin[117] (St. Marie, p. 89). Father Longobardi
notes (8: 44) that by the word Xin, the Chinese mean pure
rising spirits, and by Kuey, impure or descending spirits.
But that does not seem an exact interpretation, since Father
de S. Marie (p. 89) quotes the words of Confucius: "Oh,
the rare virtues and grand perfections of these celestial
spirits Kuei-Xin! Is there any virtue superior to them?
One does not see them, but by their actions they are made
manifest. One does not hear them, but the marvels which
they never cease to effect speak enough."[118] Confucius also
says (recorded on p. 91), that we are not able to conceive
in what manner the Spirits are so intimately united with us;

---

117. T'ien-shen 天神 , "Heavenly spirits," and kuei-shen 鬼神 ,
"ghosts and spirits," the general term for inhabitants of the spirit
world. Kuei is properly "ghosts," connoting troubled, and mischievous
entities, often demons. Shen has only favorable connotations, referring
to pure and intelligent spirits. Both terms are often used to refer to
the human souls (see fn. 153), and Leibniz, taking his cue from Ste.
Marie and Longobardi, distinguishes "subaltern spirits" from human souls
more sharply than most Chinese would have done. See §57ff. for
Leibniz's treatment of the human soul. "Genii" has been used by most
sinologists of the last century as translation for the Taoist hsien
"immortals."

118. The quotation is from the Chung Yung XVI, 1-3, where it is attributed to Confucius.

thus we cannot be hasty in honoring them or serving them or offering them sacrifices, for although their operations are secret and invisible, their benefits are visible, effective and real.[119]

§37   With such clear statements from a classical author, it seems to me that the missionaries of whom Father de S. Marie speaks (p. 90) have had good reason to compare the Spirits or the genii to our Angels. Father de S. Marie recognizes that the Chinese regarded them as subordinate to Xangti, universal and supreme Spirit of Heaven (p. 89), and he compares them (p. 96) with the ministering or inferior gods of the great God of Seneca, and of St. Augustine when he was still a Manichean, as recorded in his Confessions [Book VII, 7]. These missionaries have thus believed (with good reason, to my mind), that the most ancient Chinese philosophers, and Confucius after them, have had knowledge of the true God and of the celestial Spirits who serve Him, under the names of Xangti and Kuei-Xin. I say this because the ancient Chinese philosophers seem to ascribe to them a particular concern for defending and protecting men, cities, provinces and kingdoms, not as if they were the souls or the substantial forms of these things, but as if they were pilots of vessels -- what our philosophers call assisting intelligences and forms. And it is necessary to admit that

---

119. Ibid., XVI, 4-5, and XVII, 1-3.

the words of Confucius and other ancient authors carry the
meaning sensu maxime obvio et naturali.[120] There is a great
likelihood that these [Chinese] expressions, so close to the
great truths of our tradition, have come to the Chinese
through the tradition of the ancient Patriarchs.

§38   Father de Sainte Marie opposes only those interpreters who are called classical, but who are in fact much
later. The great Commentary on the original books called
Ta-Ziven, and the compendium of philosophy called Sing-Li
(1: 11)[121] or what Father de Sainte Marie calls the Taciven
Singli were compiled, according to this Father, by royal
order over 300 years ago, so that one may consider them as
modern. And their authority concerning the true sense of
the ancient texts is no greater than the authority of an
Accursius or a Bartolus concerning the explanation of the
meaning of the Edictum perpetuum of ancient Roman jurisprudence, which one has found today to be often quite

---

120. "In a maximally obvious and natural sense."
121. The citation (and transliteration) here is to Longobardi, not
Ste. Marie. The former's description of his sources (1: 11-12) is not
clear, so that Leibniz might well have been confused by the separation
of the names Ta-Ziven from Sing-Li, which together comprise the
Compendium. At times, Ste. Marie also reverses the title, calling it
the Taciven Singli. See Introduction, pp. 30-31. See also Mungello.

removed from these commentators.[122]   It is like several views
which the Arabs and Scholastics have ascribed to Aristotle,
which are far removed from the true sense which the ancient
Greek interpreters gave to him and which modern interpreters
have recovered.   And I believe myself to have shown what
Entelechie means, which the Scholastics scarcely understood.[123]

§39   Thus the authority that Fathers Longobardi and de
Sainte Marie ascribe to Chinese moderns is only a scholastic
prejudice.   They have judged the later Chinese school as the
medieval European school (with which they are preoccupied)
would have us judge them, namely to judge the texts of the
divine and human Laws and of ancient authors by their own

---

122. The form of the Edictum -- the decree outlining the jurisdictional
procedures, which was issued by each ancient Roman magistrate upon
entering his office -- was finally stabilized about 130 A.D. by the
jurist Salvius Julianus at the instigation of the Emperor Hadrian. This
Edictum Perpetuum ("Perpetual Edict"), alterable only by the Emperor himself, became an object of legal study in the Middle Ages, even though
the original text was lost and its contents known only through commentaries. Both Franciscus Accursius (c. 1182-1260) -- last and greatest of
the Glossators of the Bologna school of law -- and Bartolus of Saxoferrato
(1314-1357), teacher of law at Perugia and the most famous of the so-
called "Commentators" or "Post-Glossators," dealt with the Edictum Perpetuum in their writings. Both were paragons of medieval jurisprudence
for later generations, though for Leibniz, they are examples of the in-
adequacy of medieval legal studies, given the advances in understanding
Roman law in his own day.

123. See fn. 46.

interpretations and commentaries. This is a defect rather
common among philosophers, lawyers, moralists and theologians.
It is also common among medical doctors, who not yet having
a definite school, nor the same regulated language, have
gone so far in contempt of the ancients (and are so eager to
shake off such a yoke), that they have fallen into arbi-
trariness, since they have scarcely anything of established
fact beyond experience or observations, which themselves are
often not too well ascertained. Consequently it seems that
medicine has need of being entirely rebuilt on the basis of
the authoritative communications of several of its outstanding practitioners, who would re-establish a common
language, would distinguish the certain [from the possible],
would provisionally assign probabilities to the latter and
would discover a sure method of development for the
science -- but this is said simply in passing.[124]

---

124. Leibniz often attacked the scientific pretensions of the medicine
and jurisprudence of his day. He thought of medicine as an empirical
and inductive science, but nevertheless hoped that one day, after
firmly establishing certain facts through continued observation and
experimentation, it might be possible to discover certain rules or laws
which would then be the basis of establishing a rational, deductive
science of medicine. Leibniz was certain that the latter could be done
with the principles of law and often attacked those who thought of
jurisprudence as based simply on various empirical rules. See
Couturat, pp. 154-155.

§39a   The scant authority of the commentators makes it
surprising to me that very clever theologians of our time,
who prefer the doctrine of the ancient Fathers of the
Church to modern sentiment in speculative theory as well
as in morality, nevertheless pretend to judge Chinese theology through modern eyes rather than ancient ones.   One
should not find it at all surprising in a Father Longobardi
or in a Father de S. Marie, who apparently reflect the
sentiments of a vulgar theological and philosophical school.
But it seems to me that among scholarly theologians who oppose themselves to the Jesuits on this matter of Chinese
doctrine, there must be others who should be able to judge
quite otherwise.

§40   Father de S. Marie does record something in passing
which could make us suspect that the ancient [Chinese]
philosophers did not have true beliefs [i.e., consistent with
Christian doctrine].   But since he scarcely dwells on it,
I doubt that the matter can be adequately verified or made
clear.   However, I do not wish to conceal it, so I will proceed with all possible sincerity.   After having quoted
(p. 89) the fine passage of Confucius noted above, he claims
that the same author, continuing his discourse, discovers
how far his vulgar error on this point goes.   For Confucius
says (according to this Father), that the Spirits are in
truth united and incorporated with all things, from which

they are unable to separate themselves without being totally
destroyed.[125]   This opinion conforms very much (says the
Father) to the overall philosophy of Confucius, in which he
teaches that the Nature and essence of things is the Li,
Taikie, their first principle and their Creator, which as
King of Heaven is called Xangti (that is, Supreme King).
That which dominates the individual and subaltern Beings,
where generation and corruption take place, is called Kuei-
Xin. Now as matter and form cannot be separated without
the destruction of the whole unit that they constitute, in
the same way, spirits are so united to things, that they
could not leave them without their own dissolution.[126]

§41   I wanted to cite word for word the words of Father de
S. Marie which I am now going to examine. I should say at
the outset that I am inclined to believe that these are not
the express doctrines of Confucius, but opinions which have
been ascribed to him on the basis of modern interpretations.
For the actual words recorded of him do not bear this
meaning, unless one wanted to claim that he spoke under the
veil of religion simply to fool his unsophisticated readers.
But the charge that his true beliefs were those of Atheists
should only be made on the basis of solid evidence, for which

---

125. See fn. 127.
126. Leibniz uses this argument in another context in §64.

I have seen absolutely no basis until now, other than the veiled intepretations of modern commentators who would probably not dare to assert as much explicitly. If Confucius had this opinion concerning Spirits, he would not have thought any more positively of them than our ordinary Schoolmen do concerning the souls of animals -- i.e., they believe them to perish with the animal itself. But if that were so, how is it that Confucius ascribes to these Spirits and genii those rare virtues and great perfections, those marvelous operations, those grand benefits worthy of our recognition and worship?

§42   Furthermore, Confucius and the ancients ascribe Spirits and ministering genii to several things which are not at all suited for such ascriptions, for example to men, to towns and to provinces. But then, what is the likelihood of a Spirit being incorporated with its mountain, or river, or the likelihood even of the spirit of the four seasons being incorporated with the seasons themselves, or of the spirit of hot and of cold being incorporated with these qualities? Thus it must be said either that these ancient Chinese were hoodwinking the people and sought only to mislead them -- a charge one should not make without proof -- or that they believed in subaltern spirits, ministering agents of the divinity, each governing matters in his own department; or finally, that they honored, through their names, a divine quality that was suffused everywhere, as some ancient Greeks and Romans claimed that they worshipped only one Godhead, but under the names of several Gods.

§43   Furthermore, I suspect that Father de S. Marie has mistaken the meaning of Confucius when he interprets the latter as saying that spirits cannot be separated from the things they govern without being destroyed. Confucius seems rather to have said that Spirits cannot separate themselves from things without those things they are meant to govern being destroyed, for this is how I find that Father Longobardi has understood it, citing Chapter 16 of the Chung-Jung (11: 57) where Confucius, after having taught that spirits are parts which compose the being of things, adds that Spirits can be separated from them, but only with the destruction of those things (he does not say of the spirits) ensuing.[127]   Further, there is the likelihood that since Confucius made spirits parts of things, he did not mean all spirits, for the reasons I have cited [in §41 and §42]. Perhaps also the term part is taken here in a broader

---

127. Leibniz is following Longobardi's text, but they both read too much into the Chung Yung passage, which reads: 體 物 而 不 可 遺   ; "[The kuei-shen] are present in things, and may not leave them." Ste. Marie (fn. 125) must have been referring to the same passage.

sense, i.e., that which is in a thing, and is required for its subsistence of conservation.

§44   There are many Chinese moderns who claim to be followers of Confucius and the ancients, but who do not at all recognize the existence of spiritual substances, and not even of true substances, excepting matter, which they consider as alterable only by figural motions and by accidental qualities.   According to these moderns, I say, celestial or other spirits which the ancient Chinese ascribe to things are only nominal, denominating simply the mass of accidental qualities of matter, and are like the forms which make up the Beings _per accidens_ of the Schoolman,[128] i.e., a pile of stones, mountains of sand, etc. -- forms quite inferior without doubt even to the souls of beasts.   Whether one takes these souls in the manner of the Scholastics, or in the Cartesian sense (much better organized, but still a mass of accidental qualities); on either interpretation, these souls are quite removed from meriting worship, since the Spirit of Heaven, the Spirit of natural causes, the Spirit of the mountains (for example) lack organs, and consequently they would be incapable of knowledge and even of the possibility of knowledge.   Thus it would be pure deceit to want to do homage to them.

---

128.   As opposed to a Being in itself or _ens per se_, such as an animal with a soul and an organized body.   See also fns. 7 and 115.

§45   The Xu-King, one of the most ancient and seminal works
according to Father Longobardi (1: 10), recounts, Chapt. 1,
page 11 (11: 51), that since the time of Jao and of Xun[129]
(early founders of the Empire), the Chinese have revered
Spirits and that four kinds of sacrifices were made to four
kinds of Spirits. The first sacrifice, called Lui,[130] was
made to Heaven and collectively to its Spirit called Xangti.
The second, called In,[131] was made to the Spirit of the
six principle causes, i.e., the four seasons of the year,
heat, and cold, the Sun, the Moon, the stars, the rain
and dryness. The third, named Vuang,[132] was made to the
Spirit of the Mountains and of the great rivers. And the
fourth, named Pien,[133] was made to the Spirits of things
of lesser importance in the Universe, and to illustrious men of the empire. Now the same Father notes
(2: 13) that according to the text, there are different
Spirits, which he names Kuei, or Xin or jointly Kuey-Xin,[134]
which preside over the mountains, the rivers or other things

---

129. The legendary sage rulers Yao 堯 and Shun 舜 , who reigned ca.
the 24th and 23rd centuries B.C. The Shu Ching source is in Legge, vol.
III, pp. 33-34.
130. Lei 類 .
131. Yin 禋 .
132. Wang 望 .
133. P'ien 徧 .
134. Kuei-shen. See fn. 117.

in the lower world. But the [Chinese] interpreters explain
these rather as natural causes or qualities which produce
certain effects.

§46   These interpreters are correct when they do not
accept -- as the ignorant people of antiquity did -- that
Jupiter, or some aerial genie throws thunderbolts, that
there are certain greybeards, residing in the mountains and
the hollows of the earth who pour out the rivers from their
urns; they are correct when they believe that all comes
about naturally by virtue of the qualities of matter. However, the Chinese interpreters cited by Longobardi are not
correct if they believe that the ancients wanted to show
reverence to these brute objects and that they reduced the
first principle, the governor of Heaven -- or rather the
governor of the Universe -- to this same condition of a mass
of brute qualities, since the wonders of particular things,
which know not at all what they are doing, could come only
from the wisdom of the first principle. Therefore, one
must believe either that the ancient sages of China believed
that certain genii, as Ministers of the supreme Lord of
Heaven and Earth, presided over earthly things, or that they
still wanted to revere the Great God through the qualities
of individual things, under the names of the Spirits of
these things, for the benefit of popular imagination. If the
second alternative is correct, then it is in this way that

they believed that all is one; that the quality of a grand,
unique principle appears throughout the wonders of particular things, and that the Spirit of the seasons, the
Spirit of the mountains, the Spirit of the rivers, was the
same Xangti who governs Heaven.

§47   This second alternative is the truest. However, the
first view, which acknowledges genii presiding over natural
things, celestial spheres, etc., is not at all intolerable
to, nor destructive of, Christianity, as I have already re-
marked above [in §2]. It will be easy to teach and make
the Chinese receptive to that which is the most true by a
reasonable interpretation of this Axiom that the all reduces itself to the power of the one; that is, that the
powers of all inanimate creatures do not manifest their own
wisdom, but the wisdom of the Author of things and they are
only a natural consequence of forces which the first principle instills in them. It will be more difficult, however, to make them understand -- following the true
philosophy of our time -- that animated substances are potentially everywhere, but they actually exist only where
there are bodies that can perceive;[135] that these animated

---

135. See §2. The "true philosophy of our time" is, of course, Leibniz's
own. He is referring to his theory that there are an infinity of substances or monads that have life, that is, that are informed with
souls (animae) or entelechies that enable them to feel and/or perceive.

substances have their own souls or spirits as does man, and
that there is an infinity of them above as well as below
the Soul or Spirit of man. Moreover those substances which
are above, are called Angels and genii, some of which, more
specifically, serve the supreme Spirit, being more disposed
to comprehend his will and conform themselves to it; that
the souls of virtuous people are associated with them,
rendering the latter worthy of homage, but not to the destruction of one's obligations to the supreme substance.

§48   Thus one can even find satisfaction with modern
Chinese interpreters, and commend them, since they reduce
the governance of Heaven and other things to natural causes
and distance themselves from the ignorance of the masses,
who seek out supernatural miracles -- or rather super-

There are infinitesimal levels of such feelings or perceptions, each
blending into the next (Leibniz's doctrine of petites perceptions).
Some substances are endowed or "preformed" with bodily organs giving
them the potential for apperception or reflective consciousness.
Such potentialities are eventually realized in accordance with a pre-
established harmony (see §14 and fn. 48); that is, when there is a
complete correlation between the level of complexity and subtlety of
the matter and the corresponding form or soul. Leibniz believed that
this theory was the only one which explained the origin of individual
forms or souls without appealing to purely materialistic grounds (viz.,
that the soul is nothing but a particular collocation of material
atoms) or to God's consistently miraculous and ad hoc creation of new
forms or souls (see §13). The Monadology, #s 14ff and Theodicy, #91
give accounts of this central doctrine of Leibniz's mature philosophy.

corporeal ones -- as well as seek out Spirits like those of
a Deus ex machina.   And one will be able to enlighten them
further on this matter by acquainting them with the new
discoveries of Europe which give virtually mathematical
reasons for some of the great wonders of nature, and by
acquainting them with the true systems of the Macrocosm
and the Microcosm.[136]   But at the same time, it is necessary
to make them recognize, as reason demands, that these natural causes -- which render their functions so exactly at
a particular point in order to create many of the wonders
[of the world] -- could not be brought about were it not

------

136.   It is hard to know exactly what specific discoveries Liebniz is
referring to concerning the "true systems of the Macrocosm and the
Microcosm." The belief that man, the Microcosm, "mirrors the universe"
or Macrocosm (and vice versa in that both are constructed according to
the same proportions or have the same organic structure), is an ancient doctrine, with many variations, going back to the pre-Socratics.
With his characteristic immodesty, Leibniz is probably alluding to his
own doctrine, whereby "every single substance is a perpetual living
mirror of the universe" (Monadology, #56) and "every monad . . . is
representative of the universe from its own point of view, and is as
much regulated as the universe itself" (Principles of Nature and Grace
[1714], #3). The same coherent body of natural laws and the same harmony (see §14, fn. 48) pre-established by God to govern individual
substances governs the universe as a whole. In this sense, Leibniz
claims, we should understand the Chinese doctrine that "all is one";
that is, "that the quality of a grand, unique principle appears throughout the wonders of particular things" (end of §46 above).

for mechanisms prepared for, and formed by, the wisdom and
power of the supreme substance, which one may call, with
them, Li.

§48a   It is for this reason perhaps, that Confucius did
not want to explain himself concerning the Spirits of
natural things;[137] he thought that what should be revered in
the Spirit of Heaven, the seasons, the mountains, and other
inanimate things was only the supreme spirit, the Xangti,
the Taikie, the Li, but did not believe the people at all
capable of detaching this Supreme Spirit from the objects
which fell under their senses, and therefore he did not
want to expound on it. This is why, according to F. Longobardi (3: 27), in the Lunxin,[138] Chap. 3, Part 3, a disciple
of Confucius named Zuku[139] said as if in complaint of his
Master: "I never got him to speak about human nature and
the natural state of Heaven, except at the end of his life."
In the same book, Confucius says, "The proper way of
governing the people is to so act that they honor the
Spirits while distancing themselves from them." That is,

---

137. Probably a reference to Lun Yü 7: 20: "The Master would not discuss unusual occurrences, physical strength, disorder, or spirits
[shen 神]." See also fn. 42.
138. The Lun Yü. The reference should be to 5: 12.
139. Tzu-kung 子貢 (520-450? B.C.), one of the most famous disciples of Confucius. In this section Leibniz is quoting Longobardi
directly.

he refrained from wanting to examine what the Spirits are and what they do.[140] In Book 4, page 6, it is said that there were four things -- Spirit one among them -- about which Confucius maintained a great silence.[141] Commentaries state that the reason for this is because there are several matters difficult to understand, and consequently it is unseemly to speak of them to everyone. In the Book Kialu,[142] it is said that Confucius, wanting to deliver himself from the importuning queries of his disciples (who did not cease to question him about the Spirits, the rational Soul and about what happens after death), decided to give them a general rule: to argue and dispute as much as they wanted

---

140. Lun Yü 6: 20. Leibniz has interpolated the phrase "to govern the people." He then inserted, but crossed out, another anecdote from the Lun Yü, 11: 11.

141. See fn. 137.

142. Longobardi provides no source, nor context, for ascertaining the reference of "Kialu." Perhaps it is the Chia Yü 家語 -- a text of the Han Confucians -- but there is no mention of the "6 positions" in this work. On the other hand, the reference to Lun Yü 11: 11 that Leibniz crossed out above (fn. 140) concerns one of the disciples of Confucius, Chi Lu 季路 (542-479 B.C.), and this chapter fits the context of Leibniz's remarks -- except for the "6 positions": "Chi-lu asked about serving the spirits [kuei-shen]. The Master said, 'Not [yet] being able to serve mankind, how can you serve the spirits?' The disciple then asked about death. The Master said, 'Not [yet] knowing about life, how can you know about death?'" The "6 positions" are the 4 cardinal directions, zenith and nadir.

to on matters concerning the six positions, which are in the visible world (it is necessary to learn more about these six positions); however, with regard to other matters, he desired to leave them be, without discussion and without investigating them more deeply.

§49   From this Father Longobardi infers the conclusion that the literati sect possessed an esoteric doctrine reserved for the masters alone; but this does not follow at all, because Confucius himself could have been ignorant about that which he did not want to investigate more deeply.   To all appearances there is no such secret sect today in China, unless one would like to say that the Hypocrites[143] constitute one.   And even if there were such sects, one cannot rest merely on what people venture to say in their public works.   Everywhere there are some who ridicule their own dogmas.   Thus when this Father says (11: 58) that the majority of literati acknowledge living spirits or spirits of sacrifice, while prestigious literati acknowledge only spirits of generation and corruption (which are merely simple material properties), I am surprised

---

143. Like his use of "Atheist Mandarins" in §10 and "Skeptics" in §27, Leibniz probably uses "Hypocrites" here to denote those members of the Chinese intelligentsia of Ming-Ch'ing times who were elaborate but proper in the carrying out of ritual observances and sacrifices, but agnostic, or atheist, in their religious beliefs.

that the Father wants the Missionaries to pay deference
principally to these latter doctors. My own belief is
that they should regard them as heterodox, and ally themselves to common, public doctrines.

§50   Furthermore, the Father appears to conclude from
the affected silence of Confucius that Confucius himself
had wrong opinions. The father says throughout his work
that the ancient Chinese were as atheistic as the modern;
he says so expressly in section 16, page 84. He believes
that this method of Confucius corrupted the hearts and
clouded the minds of the Chinese scholars, reducing them
to thinking only about visible and palpable matters, and
that consequently they fell into the greatest of all
evils: Atheism. I would believe that this silence and
approach of Confucius contributed to it, and that he would
have done better to explain himself further; however, it
appears that the moderns have pressed the matter beyond
the limits of his method. One could say that far from
denying the existence of spirits and of religion, he simply wanted his followers not to dispute about such matters
but to content themselves with appreciating the existence
and the effects of the Xangti and the Spirits, honoring
them and practicing virtue in order to please them, without delving into their nature and without entering into
the how or the manner of their operations. Throughout our

own history, there have been Christian authors who have
given the same advice without having any evil intent.
Thus I find that everything that has been said against
the ancient Chinese to be only groundless suspicions.

§51   The common authoritative doctrine of the Chinese
on Spirits appears sufficiently well presented in a passage of their philosophy which the Father himself recounts
(12: 61ff). The Chu-zu,[144] Book 28 of the Great Philosophy,
page 2, asks: "Are Spirits made from air?" The answer
given is that it appears more likely that they are the
force, the power, and the activity in the air, rather than
the air itself. On page 13, he [Chu Hsi] distinguishes
between good spirits who possess clarity and righteousness and produce good effects in the sun, moon, day,
night, etc., on the one hand, and devious and obscure
spirits on the other. He adds a third category of spirits,
who respond to questions asked of them and grant requests
made of them.[145]   On page 38, he proves that there are spirits
by the following reasoning: if there were no spirits, the
ancients would not have made demands of them after fasting
and other abstinences. Moreover, the Emperor sacrifices
to Heaven and Earth; the Princes and Dukes (or heroes)

---

144. Longobardi is quoting a passage written by Chu Hsi -- i.e.,
"Chu-zu" -- from the Compendium.
145. See fn. 117.

sacrifice to the great rivers and grand mountains; the lords
offer five sacrifices, etc.,

§52   The same author asks further, "When one sacrifices
to Heaven, to Earth, to the mountains and the waters; when
one offers up and slaughters [animal] victims; when one
burns pieces of silk; when one offers libations of wine;
is all this done only in order to demonstrate the heart's
good intentions, or indeed because there is an Air (a
spirit) which receives the offerings? If we say that
nothing comes to receive what is offered, then to whom are
we sacrificing? And what is it on high which inspires us
with awe and which leads mankind to make sacrifices and to
be fearful? If we also say that he descends in a cloud-
chariot, it will be a great deception." It seems that this
Author wanted to hold a position midway between the skepti-
cism of the unbelievers and the crude imaginings of the
people. He desires that one recognize and honor spirits,
but that one not believe them existing in such a manner as
the imagination may represent it.

§54   [Chu Hsi] also seeks a relationship or sense of pro-
portion between the Spirit to whom one sacrifices and he
who sacrifices. That is why the Emperor must sacrifice to
the King-on-high or the Lord of Heaven, and thus he is

called Tien Zu,[146] son of Heaven. Princes and Dukes sacri-
fice to the protecting Spirits of the five ways of life.
Scholars sacrifice to Confucius in the schools of the
Universities. This relationship also requires further
that each person sacrifice to his ancestors. From this,
[Chu Hsi] wants to indicate that the Spirits govern ac-
cording to order and aid those who conform to it. Whereas
Father Longobardi concludes from these passages (12: 65)
that Spirits are made up only of air and matter, the Chinese
Author actually suggests the opposite.

§54a   I have also found another rather charming line of
reasoning against idolators in this Chinese Philosophy.
The scholar Ching-Lu[147] explains the Chung-Jung of Confucius
(Book 28, page 37) -- as reported by Father Longobardi himself (12: 60) -- saying that it is quite stupid to ask for
rain from wooden and earthen idols, which are inside
Temples, while neglecting the mountains and the waters, that
is, those things whose vapors produce the rain. He suggests that reverence should be grounded on reason, by ob-
serving the relations and proportions between things; only
then is it acceptable to the spirits, or rather to the

---

146. T'ien tzu 天子, "Son of Heaven."
147. Ch'eng I 程頤 (1033-1108), was a famous Neo-Confucian philosopher. The reference is not to the Chung Yung, but to Ch'eng I's commentary thereon in the Compendium, from which Longobardi is translating.

Xangti, to the Universal Spirit, or if you wish, to the Li,
to the supreme reason which governs all. Now the good
Father penetrates very little into [the author's] meaning
when he concludes from this that the latter recognizes the
existence of no other Spirit in the waters and mountains
than that of corporeal air, which is without consciousness.

§54b   In the same vein, Confucius says in his Su Lum Iu[148]
(by the account of Father de S. Marie, p. 29); that to
sacrifice to a spirit not of your station and situation or
not fitting for you is foolhardy and futile flattery; justice and reason find it repugnant. Now according to the
account of Chum Ko Lao,[149] it is the province only of the
Emperor to sacrifice to Heaven and Earth; only the Heroes
of the Kingdom sacrifice to the mountains and the waters;
and only illustrious men sacrifice to the Spirits; the rest
of the people are responsible for the sacrifices to their
ancestors. The Philosophical Summa [Hsing-Li] says (in F.
de S. Marie, p. 31) that souls seek Spirits of the same
quality and those with which they have the best rapport.
For example, if a peasant addressed himself to the spirit

---

148. Must be a reference to the Lun Yü, 2: 24.

149. This term appears twice in the Mission Treatise: once as CHVM
KO LAO, and once as CHAM KO LAO. In neither place is a context provided
that suggests a reference for the term. It is most probably the name
of a minor Neo-Confucian who had some of his writings, or commentaries,
included in the Compendium.

of a man of station, he would be immediately rebuffed and
the spirit would do nothing. But if someone invokes a
spirit appropriate to his station, he is assured that he
will affect the spirit and cause it to favor him. Now the
F. de S. Marie adds (p. 32) that only scholars sacrifice
to Confucius and that it is in this way that one should
understand what Father Martinius divulged in Rome in 1656,
namely that the temple, or as it is called, the Hall of
Confucius, is closed to everyone but scholars. The same
Father notes (p. 50) that Chinese soldiers revere an ancient and illustrious captain, Tai-Kung, doctors a Chinese
Asclepius, goldsmiths an ancient Alchemist, whom they call
Su-Hoang.[150]

---

150. Ste. Marie provides no more information about these figures than
Leibniz gives here, making the task of identifying them difficult,
because the Chinese pantheon of minor dieties and patron saints is
very large. "Tai-Kung" is probably the military hero of the Three
Kingdoms period Kuan Yü 關羽 , better known as Kuan Ti 關帝 or
Kuan Kung 關公 . He was one of the most popular of all heroes in
China. There are many patron saints and gods having to do with medicine,
but the "Chinese Asclepius" is probably Yao Wang 藥王 (ca. 9th
Century B.C.), whose given name was Sun Ssu-miao 孫思邈 . "Su
Hoang" is probably a reference to the 2nd Century B.C. magician Tung-
fang So 東方朔 , legendarily an incarnation of the planet Venus,
and the protector of those who work with metals. See also Werner.

§55   This father goes into further detail (p. 95). According to him, the Chinese ascribe to the very exalted
Xangti, and to all the other Spirits, Kuei-Xin, the governance of the world. The former governs as a sovereign
Lord who inhabits Heaven as his palace, and the latter
govern as his ministers, each overseeing the position
which has been entrusted to him: the Sun, moon, stars,
clouds, thunder, hail, storms and rain; earth, mountains,
lakes, rivers, crops, fruits, forests, and the grass;
humans and animals, houses, doorways, wells, kitchens,
furnaces and even the most unclean places; and still others
oversee war, the sciences, medicine, agriculture, naviga-
tion and all the technical arts. Each Chinese takes for
his Patron a spirit to whom he prays, whom he invokes, and
to whom he sacrifices in order to be treated favorably.
Each also renders to his ancestors the same obligations
rendered to familiar and domestic spirits; [non-familial]
dead are treated as strangers. They pray to Confucius and
his most renowned disciples as the Spirits who preside
over the Schools and the sciences. The Father adds that
the Chinese are like the Stoics, who pictured a material
God suffused throughout the Universe in order to move it,
and to govern it with other, subaltern gods. But I find
nothing which prevents us from finding here a spiritual
God, author of matter itself, displaying His wisdom and
power in brute things and served by intelligent spirits

similar to our own angels and souls. And one could thus
say that the average Chinese, like the pagans, multiply
individual spirits beyond measure and need, while wise men
content themselves with a belief in the Supreme spirit
and in his ministers in general, without assigning them
fixed ministries.

§56   I said at the outset that I did not want to examine
to what extent the manner of worship of the Chinese could
be condemned or justified, and that I only wanted to investigate their doctrines [end of §1]. It seems to me
(to bring everything together) that the intent of their
sages was to venerate the Li or supreme reason -- which
made itself visible and operative everywhere -- be it
directly in brute objects where intelligence is appropriate only to their author, or be it through lower spirits,
serving as ministers (with whom virtuous souls are associated). The very same sages wanted attention given to
objects in which the supreme wisdom appears more particularly, and that each one render homage in the prescribed
ways to the objects appropriate to his station. The
Emperor will render homage, and defer, to Heaven and
Earth; the great Lords to the great bodies which have an
influence in the production of food (such as the elements,
the rivers, the mountains); the scholars to the spirits
of great philosophers and legislators; and everyone to the

virtuous souls of their families. Father de S. Marie (p. 25) records an outstanding passage, where the Chinese interpreters tell us that two characters -- Ty Chang[151] -- are uttered to honor one's ancestors. Here is their explanation: when the Emperor sacrifices to his ancestors, he must elevate his spirit and reflect upon the creator from which his first ancestor is descended, and address his sacrifice to both of these united. (And not as if they were equals; this is, I believe, how one should understand it.) Father S. Marie here adds that the ancient interpretation of these characters says the same thing; that the letter Ti signifies that, in sacrificing to their ancestors, worshippers relate through their sacrifices to the origins from whence they came and to which they will return at death; always careful, however, of the order of precedence of ancestors. In other words, the souls of the ancestors are regarded as subaltern spirits to the supreme spirit and universal Lord of Heaven and Earth.

---

151. Although Ste. Marie does not cite a source, he is probably making reference to the Li Chi chapter (Legge, vol. I, pp. 223-25) in which the sacrifices of the Emperor and nobles are specified. Four of the major sacrifices related to the seasons, and those for summer and autumn were named ti 禘 and ch'ang 嘗 , which were later used together as names of the highest ancestral sacrifices. At times ti was used this way alone, as in Lun Yü 3: 10 and 3: 11. In neither of these classical texts, however, is it mentioned that the names of these sacrifices were to be uttered while performing them.

[III. Chinese Opinion Concerning the Human Soul, its Immortality, Rewards and Punishments]

§57 We have spoken of the First Principle, author and
governor of things, known under the name of the Li, Taikie
or Xangti, according to the Chinese, and then of his
ministers, the subaltern spirits called Xin, Tunxin,[152]
Kuei-Xin. To complete their theology, one has to speak of
human souls, which -- when they are separated from gross
bodies -- are called Hoën by F. Longobardi (8: 44), and
more often Ling-Hoën[153] (Preface, p. 6 and 2: 19). Sing-Hoën

---

152. This is the first (and only) mention of "Tunxin" in the Discourse.
The term does not occur in either Longobardi or Ste. Marie, and there
is no close analogue for it in this context. The two most likely can-
didates are: 1) t'u-shen 土神 , "spirits of the earth," which Ste.
Marie writes as "Tv Xin" (pp. 77 and 122); or 2) ch'ün-shen 群神 ,
the "hosts of spirits." This latter term occurs in the Shu Ching chapter discussed by Leibniz in §45. The pien sacrifice (fn. 133) was
offered to the ch'ün-shen.

153. Hun 魂 and ling-hun 靈魂 . The hun is the spiritual element
of human souls, as opposed to the p'o 魄 , or material element. The
p'o did not leave the body at death, and if the deceased was properly
buried and sacrificed to thereafter, the material soul would remain at
peace in the grave with the body, while the hun became a shen 神 ,
spirit, and aided descendents. If the body was not properly cared for,
however, the p'o left it and became a kuei (ghost), and caused mis-
chief. Ling-hun is another name for the spiritual soul, but more specifically connotes the active power, efficacy, and sphere of influence
which the spiritual soul had with respect to the descendents of the

are mentioned by Father de S. Marie (p. 58), but I suspect
a printer's error, although I am not positively certain of
this because the same Father says further on (p. 93) that
deceased men are called Sin-Kuei,[154] which he says means
retired from mortal life. It is true that for the Chinese,
souls are subsumed in some fashion under spirits, and are
integral to their worship; souls merit, however, a separate
discussion, in order to know what Chinese scholars teach
concerning the nature of these Spirits and their state
after this life.

§58   Father Longobardi asserts (2: 14) that the earliest
Chinese texts, speaking of the human soul under the name
of Ling-Hoën, lead us to understand that it endures after
the death of the body. This is why it is said in the Xi-
King,[155] Book 6, page 1, that Vuen Vuang, ancient king of
China, is on high in Heaven; he is at the side of the

---

departed. When the sacrifices to the ancestors have been minimally
neglected -- not neglected enough for the material soul to become a
kuei -- their spiritual souls would wander about, and in this state
would be called yu-hun 幽魂 (see below, fn. 156). For additional
materials dealing with the Chinese concept of the soul, especially
translations, see De Groot, vols. I and III.
154. Shen-kuei 神鬼 , reversing the order.
155. Shih Ching. See Legge, vol. IV, pp. 428-29. "Vuen Vuang" is
King Wen (fn. 102).

Xangti or the King-on-high, Lord of Heaven, and that he is
at times rising, at times descending (2: 14 and 15: 83).
The separated soul is also called Jeu-Hoën,[156] wandering
soul (ibid., p. 83), which means freely, I believe, animula
vagula blandula.[157] Doctor Paul,[158] a Christian scholar,
doubts, however (according to Father Longobardi), whether
the Chinese have any knowledge of the true God, but nevertheless believe that regarding the soul, they did have some
knowledge of it, though quite confused (17: 100). This al-
lows enough of an opening for knowledgeable missionaries
to enlighten them and to clear up their confusion. Let us
begin this task.

§59 The Chinese say (Longobardi, 15: 81) that the death
of man is only the separation of the elements of which he
is composed, and which return after this separation to the
places which are proper to them. Thus the Hoën, or soul,
rises to Heaven; the Pe,[159] or the body, returns to the

---

156. See fn. 153.
157. I.e., "wandering soul."
158. Probably Hsü Kuang-ch'i 徐光啟 , (1562-1633), Ricci's most
famous convert to Christianity. He wrote, and translated with Ricci,
works on astronomy, mathematics and agriculture. His descendants remained one of China's most influential Christian families until the present century.
159. While Leibniz refers to the physical body here, the term "Pe" is
almost surely p'o 魄 . See fn. 153.

earth. This is what is said in the Xu-King, Book I, p. 16, where the death of King Iao[160] is described in these terms: he has risen and descended. The commentary explains it in this manner; he has risen and descended means he is dead, because when a man dies, his essence of fire and air (the commentator means the animated air, the Soul) rises to Heaven, and the body returns to earth. This author speaks almost as if he had read the Holy Scriptures. So, too does the Author of the Chinese Philosophy who speaks of this matter in Book 28, about page 41, where he records this sentence of Chin-Zu:[161] when the composition of man occurs and he comes into this world -- that is, when Heaven and Earth are united -- Universal Nature does not come (for it is already present). When man dies -- that is when Heaven and Earth are separated -- Universal Nature does not leave (for it is always everywhere). But the air, which is of the essence of Heaven, returns to Heaven; and the corporeal element, which is of the essence of the earth, returns to earth.

---

160. Emperor Yao (see fn. 129). The reference to the Shu Ching does mention Yao's death, but not his "rising and descending," which was Chu Hsi's commentary on this passage. See Legge, vol. III, pp. 40-41.
161. In this section of the Compendium Ch'eng I (see fn. 147) is the author, who must therefore be the "Chin-zu" referred to here.

§60   It also appears that some Chinese scholars regard
men, and especially great men, as angels incarnate. A
certain Chinese Doctor Michael,[162] a Christian, but one
partial to Chinese doctrines, said in his preface to the
explanation of the Ten Commandments that the ancient
savants of China had been Spirits or incarnated Angels,
one succeeding the other. And with respect to the greatest
men, he goes so far as to claim that the Xangti itself or
the supreme Spirit has been incarnated in them, as for
example in the personages of Iao, of Xun, of Confucius and
of others. This is doubtlessly an error, for such an incarnation is fitting only to Jesus Christ, and his words
show well that this doctor is only quasi-Christian. But
he did not believe, however, that he would do violence to
long-standing Chinese doctrine in denying that the soul is
a fleeting and evanescent thing, [by saying that] an incarnate angel subsists before birth and after death. This
doctrine is in accord with that of Plato and Origen.[163]

---

162. Probably Yang T'ing-yun 楊廷筠 (1557-1627), another influential convert of Ricci's.

163. Plato's belief in the pre-existence of the soul, based on the
argument from recollection (ANAMNESIS) is first presented in the Meno
(81; 85D-86B) and further developed in the Phaedo (72E-77A). Though
there are scattered references throughout Plato to the soul's immortality, or rather eternality (e.g., Meno 86B; Phaedrus 245C-246A), the
main arguments are found in the Phaedo and form the bulk of this dialogue.

Another Chinese doctor, friend of the Christians, testi-
fied to Father Longobardi that he had opinions on this
matter quite close to those of Father Michael.

§61   Father de S. Marie reports (p. 76) that the Chinese
believe that Confucius and the sage kings and the ancient
philosophers of their land -- who were oracles by excellence of their virtue -- were all incarnations of God in
Heaven, Xangti, in the Kingdom of China.   The Father supports this by citing the views of some ancient philosophers,
and of the Manicheans according to Augustine, and by the
views of the Averroists and of Spinoza, who made the soul
a part or modification of God, which does not have a separate existence after death.   But on this account, great
men would have nothing over others in this respect, and
since the souls of those who are angels incarnate subsist
after death, why wouldn't the soul of one who is incom-
parably greater subsist, if God supreme is united to this
Soul and to its body in a particular fashion?

Many Church Fathers, such as Sts. Basil and Gregory, believed that
angels and other spirits were created before the material universe.
Origen in particular "was led by his strongly Platonist leanings to
affirm [the soul's] pre-existence and explained its confinement in a
body as a punishment for sins committed in its previous incorporeal
state." Article on "Soul," The Oxford Dictionary of the Christian
Church, p. 1273. See Origen, De Principiis, I, vi, 2; I, viii; I, ix.
On the immortality and ethereality of the soul, see ibid., IV, i, 36;
II, iv, 7.

§62   Thus I see nothing which prevents us from, and much
that is favorable to, our claiming rather that human souls,
according to the classical doctrine of the Chinese,
resemble the nature of Spirits, ministers of the Supreme
Spirit -- although they are to a degree inferior to them.
I am not at all surprised that Father Longobardi and Father
de S. Marie are opposed to this opinion, since heterodox
and atheistic scholars (who are permitted in China to utter
their impieties with impunity, at least orally) presented
them with strange views, current in China today, but which
are directly contrary to ancient doctrine and to religious
practices instituted over 3000 years ago in the Chinese
Empire. These [contemporary] views claim: (1) that the
Li itself (supreme Reason), or the supreme Spirit (Xangti,
as the substance of this Order or Reason) and all the intelligent Spirits which serve him are only fictions;
(2) that the supreme Spirit or universal principle is
nothing other than prime matter or corporeal air and nothing
more; (3) that the Spirits offered to the common people for
veneration are portions of this air; and (4) that all
occurs by accident or by necessity in a brutish fashion,
without any wisdom, providence or justice directing it; so
that all of Chinese religion is only a farce. But as this
imputation is ill-founded in every way, both with regard
to God and to the Angels, as we have amply demonstrated, one

may judge as well that the same obtains with respect to souls.

§63   I find nothing that these Fathers bring forth from the passages of the classical authors, from the earliest on, which sufficiently favor their allegations concerning the human soul, any more than they adduce textual support for their allegations concerning God and the angels. These Fathers give only interpretations grafted on from without, which strain or even destroy the texts and render them ridiculous, contradictory and deceitful. Father Longobardi, given what we have reported of his views -- namely, that according to the Chinese, death separates the terrestrial from the celestial, which is aerial and firelike in nature and returns to Heaven -- concludes from this that souls are something purely material which are dissolved in the air or in the ether. But by the same reasoning, one could say that Angels are nothing but fire, since God, according to Holy Scriptures, <u>fecit Ministros suos flammam ignis</u>.[164] One should rather say that these Spirits are spiritual substances, though they are clothed in subtle material bodies. So has antiquity, both pagan and Christian, ordinary conceived of the genii, Angels and Demons.

---

164. "He made a flame of fire to be His servants." A paraphrase of the Vulgate, Psalm 103, 4.

The soul returns to Heaven, and is more united than before to the celestial matter diffused everywhere, and thus more capable of conforming to the will of God, quite like the angels it resembles.[165] So have the ancient Chinese apparently understood it, when they have said that the soul is joined again to Heaven, and to the Xangti.

§64 These Fathers, or rather those who have given their impressions to the Fathers, having misused the Chinese axiom that everything is one -- i.e., that all participates in the one -- would have us believe that according to the Chinese everything is only matter but in different dispositions; that the Xangi itself is only that [i.e., matter], and so too is the Li -- "Reason" or primitive substance -- and that everything participates in matter's perfection according to its own measure of the same. Consequently, they would want the return of the soul to the Xangti to be nothing other than its dissolution into ethereal matter, it losing all knowledge gained through its bodily organs. They could say, with even more likelihood, conforming to the opinions of the Manicheans and the Averroists, that God or the Li or the Xangti is the soul of the world, which creates individual souls by acting on organic bodies, and which puts an end to them as soon as they are decomposed.

---

165. See §2 and fn. 10.

But besides the fact that these opinions are also contrary
to reason and to the nature of the individual,[166] these
opinions are also contrary to the passage from the Chinese
Author (cited by Father Longobardi) who clearly distinguishes the Universal Nature -- the Li and the Xangti --
from the particular nature of the soul. The Universal
Nature (the Chinese author says), neither comes nor goes,
but the soul comes and goes, rises and descends. That is,
it is sometimes united to a coarse body, sometimes to a more
noble one, and this gives us to understand that it continues to subsist, for otherwise it would return to the
Universal Nature.

§64a   Now let us see how Father de S. Marie speaks about
it (p. 40): the Chinese have various errors concerning
human souls. Some believe that they do not die at all,
that they simply move on and proceed to animate different
bodies, human and animal. Others believe that they
descend into Hell from whence they come out after some
time.[167] Still other Chinese acknowledge the souls as im-
mortal, claiming that they wander in the farthest mountains,
calling these souls Xin-Sien,[168] under which name they have

---

166. See §23.

167. Buddhists held the first view, and some Buddhists and many Taoists held the second.

168. Shen-hsien 神仙 , another name for "Immortals." (See fn.
108.) This was a fairly pervasive view in China.

certain chapels dedicated to them. The literati and the
better educated believe that our souls are small portions
of subtle air or a firelike and celestial vapor, detached
from the most subtle matter of Heaven from whence they
draw their origins; which, once they leave their bodies,
rise again to Heaven which is their center and from whence
they issue and where again they intermingle. The Chinese
Philosophical Summa Singlitaciven, [169] Vol. 28 -- a treatise
concerning the soul and the body -- says that the suitable
and true origin of the ethereal soul is in Heaven, to
which the ethereal soul soars [after death] to become one
and the same substance with it. The origin of the body is
the Earth into which it dissolves and transforms itself
[after death]. The author of this particular work is from
a later time and his authority does not approach that of
the ancients. However, one need not ignore this passage.
I believe that the translation of it suffers somewhat
from the prejudice of the translator [i.e., St. Marie],
when he states that the soul becomes the same substance
with Heaven. Perhaps the Chinese author only wants to say
that the two are united after death. But even if the passage were to say what [St. Marie] makes it say, such very
general expressions can always be given a [different, but

---

169. The Compendium. Leibniz is quoting Ste. Marie directly.

equally] rational meaning. For all celestial spirits are of the substance of Heaven, and the soul, becoming a celestial Spirit, becomes thereby of the same substance with Heaven. But by Heaven is understood the whole celestial Hierarchy, exercitus Coelorum,[170] under the Grand Monarch of the Universe. This Heaven is not simply the visible sky, for according to the opinions of the Chinese cited above, Heaven's air (with its celestial Spirits) extends everywhere. Thus it is not necessary, according to them, to conceive of souls as completely distinct from Heaven. To talk of wandering here and there in the mountains, rising and descending, being at the side of the Xangti, and so forth, are only imagistic ways of speaking.

§65   The [Chinese concept] of immortality of the soul will become clearer if one interprets ancient Chinese doctrine as saying that souls receive reward and punishment after this life. It is true that the literati sect [i.e., the Confucians] speak neither of Paradise nor Hell, and the Chinese Christian, Dr. Michael, regretfully acknowledges this (17: 95) in praising the sect of Foë which propounds both.[171]   It also appears that modern Chinese, who

---

170. "The Army of the Heavens."
171. Ironically, the view which Leibniz applauds here and in the next paragraph comes from Buddhism, not Confucianism.

wish to pass for being the most enlightened, ridicule this
[Buddhist] view when one talks to them of another life
(17: 89). But perhaps they will not always ridicule it if
they consider that this supreme substance -- which on their
own grounds is the source of wisdom and justice -- could
not act less perfectly on the spirits and the souls which
it creates, than a wise king in his realm acts upon his
subjects whom he did not create of his own will, and whom
it is more difficult for him to govern since they do not
depend upon him absolutely. Thus this Kingdom of the
Spirits under this great Master cannot be less orderly
than a Kingdom of men, and consequently it follows that
virtue should be rewarded and vice punished under this governance, justice being insufficiently done in this life.

§65a   This is also what the ancient Chinese have suggested. We have already noted that they place a wise and
virtuous Emperor at the side of the Xangti and that they
consider the souls of great men as angels incarnate.
Father de S. Marie (p. 27) cites the Xi-King (one of the
five principal books of the literati), which makes mention
of some of their ancient kings, who, after their death,
rise to Heaven in order to enlighten and help (I believe
this should be translated "to assist and serve") this very
exalted king Xangti, and to sit at his right and left

side.[172] It is said in the same book that these kings,
rising from the earth to Heaven, and descending from Heaven to earth, can favor and abet the Kingdom as its patrons
and protectors.[173]

§66   The worship of ancestors and great men instituted
by the ancient Chinese can indeed have for its goals, to
display the gratitude of the living as they cherish the
rewards of Heaven, and to excite men to perform actions
which render them worthy of the recognition of posterity.
However, the ancients speak as if the Spirits of virtuous
ancestors, surrounded by the aura of glory at the Court of
the Monarch of Universe, were capable of obtaining good
and evil for their descendants. And it appears by this at
least that they have conceived of them as continuing to
subsist.

§66a   It is instructive to see how they explicate this
matter. According to the account of Father de S. Marie
(p. 21ff.), Confucius makes the Emperor Xum[174] author of

---

172. This is Ste. Marie's interpretation of the same Shih Ching passage cited by Leibniz via Longobardi in §58. The "author" referred
to below is Chu Hsi.
173. Leibniz is quoting Ste. Marie directly, except for the parenthetical remark.
174. Shun. See fn. 129.

the Ancestor worship (Chung-Jung, Chpt. 17); this Emperor
was the fifth after the Foundation of the Monarchy (according to the Tung-Kien)[175] -- i.e., the Royal Chronology,
or Universal History, one of the classical texts). Confucius praises him in the extreme and attributes the
prosperity of the Empire to the worship he instituted and
also Ch. 78,[176] in which he proffers the ancient kings as
models for posterity. He also says towards the end of this
chapter that anyone who understood perfectly what the worship of Heaven and Earth comprised, and the proper reason
for sacrificing to his ancestors, would be able to assure
himself a peaceful prosperity and a wise government throughout the kingdom with as much certainty as if he held them
in his very hand.[177]

§67   It is true that the Chinese scholars speak neither
of Hell nor of purgatory, but it is possible that some among

---

175. The Tzu-chih t'ung-chien 資治通鑑 , known as the Comprehensive Mirror, is a major history of China written by the famous scholar
and statesman, Ssu-ma Kuang 司馬光 , (1018-1086). It is not clear
from Longobardi's text that he has used this work, however. More probably he was using the T'ung-chien kang-mu 通鑑綱目 , --
Outline of the Comprehensive Mirror -- an abridgement of Ssu-ma Kuang's
work by Chu Hsi.

176. Ste. Marie and Leibniz have 78 here, but it should be 19.

177. This well known example can also be found in Lun Yü 3: 11, and in
the Li Chi (Legge, vol. II, p. 272).

them believe or have believed at other times that the wandering souls which prowl here and there in the mountains
and the forests are in a sort of purgatory. We have already spoken of these wandering souls.[178] Without making
too much of a comparison between the opinions of the Christians and the pagans, one could nevertheless say that
there is something approaching this in the life of St.
Conrad, a Bishop of Constance, whose biography is published
in the second volume of my collection,[179] where it is recorded that he and his friend St. Udalric discovered souls
in the form of birds condemned to the waterfalls of the
Rhine which they saved by their prayers. So too, perhaps,
according to some of these Chinese literati, ancient or
modern, souls deserving of punishment become spirits
destined to lowly stations, guarding doors and tending
kitchens and furnaces until they have expiated themselves.
We are not sufficiently conversant with the doctrine of
the scholars on these matters to go into detail about them.

---

178. In §58 and §64a.

179. Scriptores Rerum Brunsvicensium. Hanover: N. Foerster, vol.
II, 1710, pp. 7-8.

[IV. Concerning the Characters which Fohi,[180] Founder of the Chinese Empire, used in His Writings and Binary Arithmetic]

§68 It is indeed apparent that if we Europeans were well enough informed concerning Chinese Literature, then, with the aid of logic, critical thinking, mathematics and our manner of expressing thought -- more exacting than theirs -- we could uncover in the Chinese writings of the remotest antiquity many things unknown to modern Chinese and even to other commentators thought to be classical. Reverend Father Bouvet and I have discovered the meaning, apparently truest to the text, of the characters of Fohi, founder of the Empire, which consist simply of combinations of un-broken and broken lines, and which pass for the most an-cient writing of China in its simplest form. There are 64 figures contained in the book called Ye Kim,[181] that is, the Book of Changes. Several centuries after Fohi, the Emperor Ven Vam[182] and his son Cheu Cum, and Confucius more than five

---

180. Fu Hsi. See the Introduction, pp. 17-18, 22. See also fn. 79 from the text.

181. I Ching.

182. Again, King Wen; this time the spelling is Bouvet's. "Cheu Cum" is Chou Kung 周公 , the Duke of Chou and King Wen's brother. He was one of Confucius' favorite culture heroes.

centuries later, have all sought therein philosophical mys-
teries. Others have even wanted to extract from them a
sort of Geomancy and other follies. Actually, the 64
figures represent a Binary Arithmetic which apparently this
great legislator [Fohi] possessed, and which I have redis-
covered some thousands of years later.

§68a   In Binary Arithmetic, there are only two signs, 0
and 1, with which one can write all numbers.[183]   When I communicated this system to the Reverend Father Bouvet, he
recognized in it the characters of Fohi, for the numbers 0
and 1 correspond to them exactly[184] if we put a broken line
for 0 and an unbroken line for the unity, 1. This Arithmetic furnishes the simplest way of making changes, since
there are only two components, concerning which I wrote a
small essay in my early youth, which was reprinted a long
time afterwards against my will.[185]   So it seems that Fohi

---

183. At this point Leibniz wrote, but then crossed out the following:
"I have since found that it further expresses the logic of dichotomies
which is of the greatest use, if one always retains an exact opposition
between the numbers of the division."

184. At this point, Leibniz wrote, but then crossed out the following:
"provided that one places before a number as many zeroes as necessary
so that the least of the numbers has as many lines as the greatest."

185. In a letter to Remond in July, 1714 Leibniz wrote about: "a little schoolboyish essay called 'On the Art of Combinations,' published in
1666, and later reprinted without my permission." Gerhardt, vol. III,
p. 620. See also Loemker, vol. II, pp. 1067-68.

had insight into the science of combinations, but the
Arithmetic having been completely lost, later Chinese have
not taken care to think of them in this [arithmetical] way
and they have made of these characters of Fohi some kind of
symbols and Hieroglyphs, as one customarily does when one
has strayed from the true meaning (as the good Father
Kirker has done with respect to the script of the Egyptian
obelisks of which he understands nothing).[186]   Now this
shows also that the ancient Chinese have surpassed the modern ones in the extreme, not only in piety (which is the
basis of the most perfect morality) but in science as well.

§69 Since this Binary Arithmetic, although explained in
the Miscellany of Berlin,[187] is still little known, and mention of its parallelism with the characters of Fohi is
found only in the German journal of the year 1705 of the
late Mr. Tenzelius,[188] I want to explain it here -- where it

---

186. Athanasius Kircher (1601-1680), a German Jesuit scholar interested
in mathematics, Hebrew, hieroglyphics and archaeology. He is credited
with inventing the magic lantern. In Lach (2), Jean Baruzi is cited as
saying that Kircher corresponded with Leibniz about China as early as
1670 (p. 439).

187. "De periodis columnarum in serie numerorum progressionis Arithmeticae Dyadice expressorum," by P. Dangicourt, in Miscellanea Berlinen-
sia, I (1701), 336-376. This and the Tenzel article cited below (fn.
188) were both instigated by Leibniz himself. See Zacher, p. 1.

188. "Erklärung der Arithmeticae binariae, ...," in Curieuse bib-
liothec oder Fortsetzung der Monatlichen Unterredungen einiger guten

appears to be very appropriate -- since it concerns justification of the doctrines of the ancient Chinese and their
superiority over the moderns.[189] I will only add before
turning to this matter that the late Mr. Andreas Müller,[190]
native of Greiffenhagen, Provost of Berlin, a man of
Europe, who without ever having left it, had studied the
Chinese characters closely, and published with notes, what
Abdalla Beidavaeus wrote on China. This Arab author remarks that Fohi had found a peculiare scribendi genus
Arithmeticam, contractus et Rationaria, a peculiar manner
of writing, of arithmetic, of contracts, and of accounts.[191]
What he says confirms my explanation of the characters of
this ancient philosopher-king whereby they are reduced to
numbers.

Freunde , ed., W.E. Tenzel (Frankfurt and Leipzig,1705), pp. 81-112.
See Zacher, p. 210.

Leibniz omits mention of his own, earlier endeavor concerning binary
arithmetic and its relationship to the characters of Fu Hsi, written
in 1703: "Explication de l' Arithmetique Binaire qui se sert des seuls
caracteres 0 et 1; avec des Remarques sur son utilité, et sur ce
qu'elle donne le sens des anciennes figures Chinoises de Fohi," par M.
Leibniz, Histoire de l'Academie Royale des Sciences, Année 1703; avec
les Memoires . . . pour la même Année, Paris 1705 [Mem.], pp. 85-89.
A more readable and available edition of this work is found in Zacher,
pp. 293-301.

189. See Introduction, p. 37.

190. 1630?-1694. For a study of Müller on China, see Lach (3).

191. The hexagrams were never used for this purpose; Leibniz is quoting
directly from Tenzel. See also Zacher, p. 159.

§70   The ancient Romans made use of a mixed arithmetic,
quinary and denary, and one still sees reminders of it in
their counters.[192]   One sees, from Archimedes' work on the
counting of the sand,[193] that already in his time something
approaching denary arithmetic was understood (which has
come down to us from the Arabs and which appears to have
been brought from Spain, or at least made more known by
the renowned Gerbert, later Pope, under the name of
Sylvester II).[194]   This prevalence of base 10 arithmetic
seems to come from the fact that we have 10 fingers, but
as this number is arbitrary, some have proposed counting

---

192. Leibniz is talking of the Roman numerals, which except for unity
(I), are based on either five (V, L, D) or ten (X, C, M), hence the
mixed nature of their numeration or counting, but not necessarily of
their arithmetic, about which little is known. The purpose of the
Roman counters, originally pebbles (calculi), is uncertain; it has been
argued that they were used in games such as backgammon or checkers, or
even like poker chips. See Smith, vol. II, pp. 165-66.

193. "Archimedes saw the defects of the Greek number system, and in
his Sand Reckoner he suggested an elaborate scheme of numeration, ar-
ranging the numbers in octads, or the eighth powers of ten." Ibid.,
vol. I, 113.

194. Gerbert, who was Pope from 999 to 1003, has traditionally been
held responsible for introducing the Arabic numerals into Christian
Europe, which he probably learned while studying in Spain. Leibniz is
wrong in thinking that Gerbert introduced the decimal or denary system,
rather than simply the nine characters. "He probably did not know of
the zero, and at any rate he did not know its real significance."
Ibid., vol. II, 74-75; see also, Ibid., vol. I, 195-196.

by dozens, and dozens of dozens, etc.[195]   On the other hand,

the late Mr. Erhard Weigelius resorts to a lesser number

predicated on the quaternary or Tetractys like the

Pythagoreans;[196] thus, just as in the decimal progression we

write all numbers using 0, 1, 2, 3, 4, 5, 6, 7, 8, 9, he

would write all numbers in his quaternary progression using

0, 1, 2, 3; for example 321 for him signifies $3x4^2 + 2x4^1 + 1$ or

rather 48+16+1, that is 65 according to the ordinary system.

§71   This gives me the opportunity to point out that all

numbers could be written by 0 and 1 in the binary or dual

progression. Thus:

---

195. Leibniz himself toyed briefly with a base 12 (and even mentioned
a base 16) number system and may have gotten the idea from Pascal.
See Zacher, pp. 17-21.

196. Erhard Weigel (1625-1699) was professor of Mathematics at the
University of Jena, where Leibniz followed his lectures for one semes-
ter in 1663. Having been influenced strongly by the Pythagorean and
other mystical traditions in mathematics, Weigel saw the number 4 as
the perfect number and constructed a base 4 number system. Although
Weigel influenced Leibniz in many areas (e.g., the need for linguistic and legal reforms in Germany), the latter saw no need for such a
number system. Practically, a base 10 or even higher number system
(12 or 16) shortened calculations and condensed enumeration; theore-
tically, a base 2 system was best, since it had the simplest and most
easily analyzable base. Couturat, pp. 473-474.

1	1			10 is equal to 2
10	2			100 is equal to 4
100	4			1000 is equal to 8
1000	8			etc.
10000	16			
100000	32			
1000000	64			

And accordingly, numbers are expressed as follows:

These terms correspond with the hypothesis;
for example:

111=100+10+1=4+2+1=7

11001=10000+1000+1=16+4+1=25 [197]

They can also be found by continual addition of
unity, for example:

The points denote
unity which is
kept in mind in [198]
ordinary calculation.

$$\begin{array}{r} 1 \\ .1 \\ \hline 10 \\ 1 \\ \hline 11 \\ ..1 \\ \hline 100 \\ 1 \\ \hline 101 \\ .1 \\ \hline 110 \\ 1 \\ \hline 111 \\ ..1 \\ \hline 1000 \end{array}$$

0	0
1	1
10	2
11	3
100	4
101	5
110	6
111	7
1000	8
1001	9
1010	10
1011	11
1100	12
1101	13
1110	14
1111	15
10000	16
10001	17
10010	18
10011	19
10100	20
10101	21
10110	22
10111	23
11000	24
11001	25
11010	26
11011	27
11100	28
11101	29
11110	30
11111	31
100000	32
etc.	etc.

197. The mistake is Leibniz's; 4 should be 8.

198. See §72 for explanation.

§71a   But, to continue, if one wishes to make a table expressing terms for all the natural numbers in order, one
need not calculate, since it is sufficient to note that
each column is periodic, the same periodicity recurring
ad infinitum: the first column runs 0, 1, 0, 1, 0, 1, etc.;
the second 0, 0, 1, 1, 0, 0, 1, 1, etc; the third 0, 0, 0,
0, 1, 1, 1, 1, 0, 0, 0, 0, 1, 1, 1, 1, etc.; the fourth
0, 0, 0, 0, 0, 0, 0, 0, 1, 1, 1, 1, 1, 1, 1, 1, 1, 0, 0, 0, 0,
0, 0, 0, 0, 1, 1, 1, 1, 1, 1, 1, 1, etc. And so on with
further columns, assuming that the empty places above each
column are filled with zeroes. Thus one can write these
columns at once and accordingly make up the table of
natural numbers without any calculation. This is what one
can call enumeration.

§72   As for addition, it is simply done by counting and
making periods when there are numbers to add together,
adding up each column as usual, which will be done as follows: count the unities of the column; for example, for
29, look how this number is written in the table, to wit,
by 11101; thus you write 1 under the column and put periods
under the second, third and fourth column thereafter.
These periods denote that it is necessary to count out one
unity further in the column following.

§73 Subtraction is just as easy. Multiplication is reduced to simple additions and has no need of the Pythagorean

table, it sufficing to know that 0 times 0 is 0, that 0
times 1 is 0, that 1 times 0 is 0, and that 1 times 1 is 1.

§74   In division there is no need to tally as in ordinary
calculation. One must only see if the divisor is greater
or lesser than the preceding remainder. In the first case,
the sign of the quotient is 0, in the second case it is 1;
the divisor may be subtracted from the preceding remainder
to get another remainder.

§75   These are simplifications that have been proposed
by a clever man since the introduction of this Arithmetic
into certain calculations.[199] But the principal utility of
this binary system is that it can do much to perfect the
science of numbers, because all calculations are made according to periodicity. It is some achievement that the
numerical powers of the same order, made by raising the
ordered natural numbers, however high the order, never have
a greater number of periods than the natural numbers themselves which are their roots . . . . [Text breaks off at
this point.]

---

199. Leibniz is referring to Arithmeticus perfectus, Qui Tria numerare
nescit, seu Arithmetic dualis (Prague, 1712) by W.J. Pelican. Pelican
apparently showed how one can use the binary system for other calculations as well, i.e., fractional arithmetic, roots and proportions.
See Zacher, p. 211.

APPENDIX

VARIANT READINGS OF TEXT

What follows is a list of all the variant readings where the autograph differs from the best printed text, i.e., the Loosen-Vonessen edition. Paragraph numbers follow that edition. We have not noted the many
instances where Loosen-Vonessen have either added or corrected the page
numbers Leibniz noted in referring to the texts of Longobardi and Sainte-
Marie.

Paragraph:
   §1: for "considerable de son temps," read "considerable en son temps"
   §2: for "Philosophes et les Peres," read "Philosophes et Peres"
   §2: for "ressemblent à ces Chrestiens," read "ressemblent à des Chres-
       tiens"
   §2: for "ou Anges ne nient," read "ou Anges avec des anciens peres ou
       philosophes ne nient"
   §3: for "on ne pourra pas luy," read "on ne pourra luy"
   §3: for "n'etant point encore fait," read "n'etant point fait encore"
   §11: for "se contredisent. Mais," read "se contredisent veritables. Mais"
   §11: for "refutant et rebutant," read "refutant et faison [?] rebutant"
   §11: for "la plus uniforme," read "la plus raisonnable"
   §13: for "legerement toutes leurs Ecoles," read "legerement toute leur
       Ecole"
   §16: for "(ouvrage des plus ordinaires hez," read (ouvrage des plus
       originaires chez"
   §16: for "une traduction bien," read "une transaction bien"
   §17: for "et qui entendoit parfaitement," read "et qui savoit parfaite-
       ment"
   §18: for "en les expliquant de," read "en l'expliquant de"
   §20: for "qu'il n'y en a point de," read "qu'il n'y a point de"

§21: for "directrice et productice," read "directrice et productrice"

§30: for "souiller les vertus et les perfections," read "souiller les perfections"

§32: for "autant de systemes du Monde," read "autant de systemes Mondains"

§34: for "Hiaxi," read "Hia Xi"

§34a: for "qu'il avoit eue avec," read "qu'il a eue avec"

§35: for "il confondoit des choses differents," read "il confondoit des different choses"

§38: for "par ordre du Roy," read "par ordre Royal,"

§38: for "il y a plus de 300 ans," read "il y a quelques plus de 300 ans"

§39: for "separeroient l'incertain du certain," read "separeroient le certain"

§41: for "cela étant, ainsi que seroit-ce," read "cela étant, que ce seroit ce que"

§43: for "des esprits) ne s'ensuive. Et," read "des esprits) s'ensuive. Et"

§48: for "des Machines preparées pour cela," read "des Machines preparées à cela"

§48a: for "parce qu'il jugeoit," read "parce qu'ils jugeoit"

§50: for "en conclure encore, que," read "en conclure encore de ce silence affecté de Confucius, que"

§53: for "activité ou son influence," read "activité ou influence"

§54a: for "ou si vous voulés au Li," read "ou si voulés au Li"

§54b: for "peuple a le droit de sacrifier," read "peuple a droit de sacrifier"

§55: for "comme son palais," read "comme à son palais"

§55: for "terre, sur les montagnes," read "terre, les montagnes"

§55: for "favorable par des Sacrifices," read "favorable par ses Sacrifices"

§55: for "que les sages se contentent," read "que sages se contentent"

§63: for "de Dieu, de même que les Anges," read "de Dieu, tout comme les Anges"

§64: for "que selon les Chinois," read "que tout selon les Chinois"

§74: for "qu'on talonne comme," read "qu'on tatonne comme." [See Zacher, p. 210, n. 378.]

Loosen and Vonessen regularly, but not uniformly, include in brackets brief passages which Leibniz crossed-out in the manuscript. On only three occasions did we believe the crossed out material added to an understanding of the text. See textual footnotes 18, 183, and 184.

SELECTED BIBLIOGRAPHY

Note: Standard philosophical works, including those of Leibniz, are cited in the notes, but are not listed below except when a quotation was taken from a particular edition.

Allen, D., (ed.), Leibniz: Theodicy (Abridged). Indianapolis: Bobbs-
    Merrill, 1966.

Beck, L.W., Early German Philosophy. Cambridge: Harvard University
    Press, 1969.

Benoit, C., and others, trans.,"The Leibniz-Bouvet Correspondence." Bur-
    lington, Vt.

Bernard, Henri, "Chu Hsi's Philosophy and Its Interpretation by Leibniz,"
    in T'ien Hsia Monthly, volume V, no. 1, 1937.

Bodde, Derk, "Harmony and Conflict in Chinese Philosophy," in Studies in
    Chinese Thought, ed. Arthur F. Wright. Chicago: University of
    Chicago Press, 1953.

Chan Wing-tsit, "The Evolution of the Neo-Confucian Concept of Li As
    Principle," in the Tsing Hua Journal of Chinese Studies, new series,
    volume IV, no. 2, 1964.

Collins, J., The Thomistic Philosophy of the Angels. Washington: Catho-
    lic University of America Press, 1947.

Couturat, Louis, La Logique de Leibniz. Hildesheim: Olms, 1961.

Creel, Herrlee G., "Was Confucius Agnostic?" T'oung Pao, volume XXIX,
    1932.

Cross, F.L. (ed.), The Oxford Dictionary of the Christian Church. London:
    Oxford University Press, 1954.

deBary, Wm. T., "Some Common Tendencies in Neo-Confucianism," in Confu-
    cianism in Action, ed. David S. Nivison and Arthur F. Wright.
    Stanford: Stanford University Press, 1959.

De Groot, J.J.M., The Religious System of China, 6 vols. Taipei: Ch'eng-wen Reprint Co., 1969.

d'Elia, Pasquale, Galileo in China. Cambridge: Harvard University Press, 1960.

Dutens, Ludovici, ed., G.G. Leibnitii: Opera Omnia, 6 vols. Geneva: Fratres de Tournes, 1768.

Eckert, H., G.W. Leibniz' Scriptores Rerum Brunsvicensium. Entstehung und Historiographische Bedeutung. Frankfurt: V. Klostermann, 1971.

Edwards, P., (ed.), The Encyclopedia of Philosophy, 8 vols. New York: Macmillan, 1967.

Fingarette, Herbert, Confucius - The Secular as Sacred. New York: Harper and Row, 1972.

Fung Yu-lan, History of Chinese Philosophy, 2 vols., trans. Derk Bodde. Princeton: Princeton University Press, 1952.

Gerhardt, Carl, ed., Die philosophischen Schriften von G.W. Leibniz, 7 vols. Berlin: Weidmannsiche Buchhandlung, 1875-1890.

Goodrich, Anne S., The Peking Temple of the Eastern Peak. Nagoya: Monumenta Serica, 1964.

Hoffman, E., and Klibansky, R. (eds.), Nicolaus Cusanus: De Docta Ignorantia. Leipzig: F. Meiner, 1932.

Karlgren, Bernhard (1), Grammata Serica. Taipei: Ch'eng-wen Reprint Co., 1966.

_____ (2), trans. The Book of Documents. Stockholm: Museum of Far Eastern Antiquities, 1950.

_____ (3), trans. The Book of Odes. Stockholm: Museum of Far Eastern Antiquities, 1950.

Keightley, David, Sources of Shang History: The Oracle-Bone Inscriptions of Bronze Age China. Berkeley: University of California Press, forthcoming.

Kortholt, Christian, ed., Leibnitii Epistolae ad diversos. Leipzig: B.C. Breitkopf, 1735.

Lach, Donald F., ed. (1) The Preface to Leibniz' NOVISSIMA SINICA. Honolulu: University of Hawaii Press, 1957.

_____ (2), "Leibniz and China," in Journal of the History of Ideas, volume VI, 1945.

_____ (3), "The Chinese Studies of Andreas Müller," in the Journal of the American Oriental Society, volume LX, 1940.

Legge, James, trans. The Chinese Classics, 2nd rev. ed., 7 vols. Shanghai, 1894.

_____ (2), Li Chi: Book of Rites, 2 vols., with a new Introduction by C. and W. Chai. New Hyde Park: University Books, 1967.

Loemker, L., Philosophical Papers and Letters, 2 vols. Chicago: University of Chicago Press, 1956.

Longobardi, Nicholas, De Confucio Ejusque Doctrina Tractatus. Paris, 1701. (In Dutens and Kortholt).

Malebrance, Nicholas,"A Dialogue Between a Christian Philosopher and a Chinese Philosopher: On the Nature and Existence of God,"trans. by George Stengren. Mt. Pleasant, Mich.

Merkel, F.R., G.W. Leinbiz und die China-Mission. Eine Untersuchung über die Anfänge der protestantische Missionsbewegung. Leipzig: Hinrichs, 1920.

Meyer, R.W., Leibnitz and the Seventeenth-Century Revolution. Cambridge, England: Bowes and Bowes, 1952.

Morrow, G. (trans.), Plato's Epistles. Indianapolis: Bobbs-Merrill, 1962.

Mungello, David, Leibniz and Neo-Confucianism: The Search for Accord. Honolulu: University Press of Hawaii, forthcoming.

Needham, Joseph, Science and Civilization in China, 7 volumes, in progress. Cambridge: Cambridge University Press, 1954 -.

New Catholic Encyclopaedia, 16 vols. New York: McGraw-Hill, 1967.

Parkinson, G.H., (ed.), Leibniz: Philosophical Writings (rev. ed.).
    London: J.M. Dent, 1973.

Peters, F.E., Greek Philosophical Terms, A Historical Lexicon. New York:
    New York University Press, 1967.

Quasten, J., Patrology, 3 vols. Utrecht: Spectrum, 1950.

Riley, P., "An Unpublished Lecture by Leibniz on the Greeks as Founders
    of Rational Theology: Its Relation to His 'Universal Jurispru-
    dence'." Journal of the History of Philosophy, volume XIV, no. 2.

Rolt, C.E., Dionysius the Areopagite on the Divine Names and The Mystical
    Theology. New York: Macmillan, 1951.

Rosemont, Henry, Jr., "Review Article: Herbert Fingarette's Confucius -
    The Secular as Sacred," in Philosophy East and West, vol. 26, no.4,
    1976.

Ste. Marie, Antonio C., Traite sur quelques points importants de la
    Mission de la Chine. Paris, 1701. (In Dutens and Kortholt).

Schneweis, E., Angels and Demons according to Lactantius. Washington:
    Catholic University of America Press, 1944.

Schwartz, Benjamin, "Some Polarities in Confucian Thought," in Confu-
    cianism in Action, ed. David S. Nivison and Arthur F. Wright.
    Stanford: Stanford University Press, 1959.

Sivin, Nathan, "Copernicus in China," Studia Copernicana, vol. 6, 1973.

Smith, D.E., History of Mathematics, 2 vols. Boston: Ginn and Co.,
    1925.

Van Den Wyngaert, A., ed. Sinica Franciscana, 16 vols. Collegium
    S. Bonaventurae, 1929-1936.

Waley, Arthur (1), "Leibniz and Fu Hsi," in the Bulletin of the London
    School of Oriental Studies, volume II, 1921.

_____ trans. (2), The Book of Songs. New York: Grove Press, 1960.

_____ trans. (3), The Analects of Confucius. New York: Modern Library, n.d.

Werner, E.T.C., ed., Dictionary of Chinese Mythology. Shanghai: Kelly and Walsh, Ltd., 1932.

Wiener, Philip P., ed., Leibniz: Selections. New York: Charles Scribner's Sons, 1951.

Wilhelm, Hellmut, (1) "Leibniz and the I Ching," in Collectanea Commissiones Synodalis, no. 16, 1943.

_____ (2), Change: Eight Lectures on the I Ching. New York: Pantheon Books, 1960.

Wilhelm, Richard, The I Ching or Book of Changes, translated into English by Cary F. Baynes. New York: Pantheon Books, 1962.

Wittkower, R., Architectural Principles in the Age of Humanism. New York: Random House, 1965.

Wright, Arthur F., Buddhism in Chinese History. New York: Atheneum, 1965.

Zacher, H.J., Die Hauptschriften zur Dyadik von G.W. Leibniz. Ein Beitrag zur Geschichte des binären Zahlensystems. Frankfurt: V. Klostermann, 1973.

Zeller, E., Outlines of the History of Greek Philosophy (13th ed. rev.). New York: Meridian Books, 1955.

_____ (2) The Stoics, Epicureans and Sceptics. (Rev. ed.; New York: Russell and Russell, 1962.

Zempliner, Arthur, "Gedanken über die erste deutsche Übersetzung von Leibniz' Abhandlung über die chinesische Philosophie," in Studia Leibnitiana, volume II, 1970.

INDEX

Accommodationism: advocated by Ricci, 11; attacked by Longobardi, 11-12; attacked by others, 12

Accursius, Franciscus, 116-117

Ancestors: sacrifices to, 138, 139-140; neglect of, 141n; worship of, 154.

Angels: compared to Chinese spirits, 35, 115; as spiritual substances, 55-56, 58, 148; Leibniz on, 56n; place of, 127; great men as incarnations of, 145-146, 153. See also Spirits

Animals, souls of, 112, 121, 123

Aquinas, St. Thomas, 93

Arabs, arithmetic of, 161

Archimedes, 161

Aristophanes, 105

Aristotle, 117; on celestial spheres, 58; on entelecheia, 76n; on Parmenides and Melissus, 87, 88n

Arithmetic: binary, 158; Roman, mixed, 161. See also Binary arithmetic

Atheism, ascribed to Chinese, 34, 120-121, 132

Augustine, St., 55n-56n, 115, 146

Averroists (Averroism), 69, 90, 146, 149

Bartolus of Saxoferrato, 116-117

Beidavaeus, Abdalla, 160

Benedict XIV, 13

Binary Arithmetic: and trigrams of I Ching, 14, 16, 22-23, 157-158; in Discourse, 36, 37; Leibniz on, 158-162; explained, 162-165

Bouvet, Joachim, 8; career of, 13-14; theories of, 14-16, 49; on the I Ching, 22-23, 36,46; on Patriarchs, 94n; on characters of Fu Hsi, 157

DANIEL J. COOK studied at Haverford College and Columbia University (Ph.D., Philosophy, 1968), and has done post-doctoral research in West Germany. He has published articles and reviews of Leibniz and Hegel in several philosophical journals, and is the author of Language in the Philosophy of Hegel. His teaching career has been with the City University of New York: first with Herbert H. Lehman College, and currently at Brooklyn College, where he is Associate Professor in the New School of Liberal Arts.

HENRY ROSEMONT, JR. studied at the University of Washington (Ph.D., Philosophy, 1967), did post-doctoral work in linguistics at MIT, is a Research Fellow at Harvard University, and has taught at Oakland University, the University of Illinois, and the City University of New York. He is Review Editor of Philosophy East & West, and President of the Society for Asian and Comparative Philosophy (1976-78). In addition to articles in professional journals he has published, with Walter Feinberg, Work, Technology and Education. He is currently Professor of Philosophy at St. Mary's College of Maryland.